Alexander William Kinglake

The Invasion of the Crimea Its Origin, and an Account of Its Progress Down to the Death of Lord Raglan

Alexander William Kinglake

The Invasion of the Crimea Its Origin, and an Account of Its Progress Down to the Death of Lord Raglan

ISBN/EAN: 9783742801609

Manufactured in Europe, USA, Canada, Australia, Japa

Cover: Foto ©ninafisch / pixelio.de

Manufactured and distributed by brebook publishing software (www.brebook.com)

Alexander William Kinglake

The Invasion of the Crimea Its Origin, and an Account of Its Progress Down to the Death of Lord Raglan

THE
INVASION OF THE CRIMEA:

ITS ORIGIN,
AND
AN ACCOUNT OF ITS PROGRESS
DOWN TO THE DEATH OF
LORD RAGLAN.

BY
ALEXANDER WILLIAM KINGLAKE.

COPYRIGHT EDITION.

WITH ALL THE PLANS, MAPS AND EMENDATIONS
OF THE THIRD LONDON EDITION.

VOL. II.

LEIPZIG

BERNHARD TAUCHNITZ

1863.

The Right of Translation is reserved.

CONTENTS

OF VOLUME II.

TRANSACTIONS WHICH BROUGHT ON THE WAR.

CHAPTER XIV.
(Continued.)

	Page
The massacre of the Boulevard,	1
Slaughter in Central Paris,	10
Slaughter of prisoners,	11
Mode of dealing with some of the prisoners at the Prefecture,	13
Gradations by which slayers of vanquished men may be distinguished,	13
Slaughter ranging under all these categories caused by the confederates,	16
Inquiry as to the alleged shooting of prisoners who were in the hands of the civil power,	16
Uncertainty as to the number of people killed,	21
Total loss of the army in killed,	22
Effect of the massacre upon the people of Paris,	22
Effect of the massacre in removing one of Louis Bonaparte's personal disqualifications,	24
The fate of the provinces,	25
Motives for the ferocity of the measures taken,	27
Terror, and afterwards a hope of gaining support from men afraid of anarchy,	27
General dread of the Socialists,	27
The brethren of the Elysée take advantage of this,	28
They pretend to be engaged in a war against Socialism,	28
Support thus obtained,	29
Commissaries sent into the provinces,	29
The Church,	30

	Page
France disarmed,	32
Twenty-six thousand five hundred men transported,	33
The Plebiscite,	35
Causes rendering free election impossible,	35
The election under martial law,	36
Violent measures taken for coercing the election,	36
Contrivance for coercing the election by the vote of the army,	39
France succumbs,	39
Prince Louis sole lawgiver of France,	40
The laws he gave her,	40
Importance of the massacre on the Boulevard,	40
Inquiry into its cause,	40
The passion of terror,	41
State of Prince Louis Bonaparte during the period of danger,	43
He gives all he has to the soldiers,	44
He even signed the decree of the 5th of December,	46
State of Jerome Bonaparte,	46
Natural anxiety of Napoleon, son of Jerome,	47
Bodily state of Maupas,	47
Grounds for the anxiety of the plotters and of Magnan, &c.,	48
Effect of anxious suspense upon French troops,	48
Surmised cause of the massacre,	50
Gratitude due to Fleury,	52
The use the Elysée made of France,	53
The oath which the President had taken,	53
His added promise as "a man of honour,"	53
The Te Deum,	54
The President becomes Emperor of the French,	56
The inaction of great numbers of Frenchmen,	56
Its cause,	56
The gentlemen of France resolve to stand aloof from the Government,	57
The constant peril in which the confederates were kept,	58
The foreign policy of France used to prop the new throne,	58

CHAPTER XV.

Immediate effect of the Coup d'Etat upon the tranquillity of Europe,	60
The policy which it necessitated,	60

CONTENTS OF VOLUME II.

	Page
The French Government coerces the Sultan into measures offensive to Russia,	61
And then seeks an alliance with England,	61
Personal feelings of the new Emperor,	62
The French Emperor's scheme for superseding the concord of the four Powers,	62
The nature of the understanding of Midsummer 1853 between France and England,	68
Announcement of it to Parliament,	74
Failure of Parliament to understand the real import of the disclosure,	74
The Queen's Speech, August 1853,	74
This marks where the roads to peace and war branch off,	75

CHAPTER XVI.

Count Nesselrode,	77
State of the Czar after learning that the fleets of France and England were ordered to the mouth of the Dardanelles,	78
His complaints to Europe,	79
Their refutation,	79
The Vienna Conference,	80
The effect upon England of becoming entangled in a separate understanding with France,	81
The French Emperor's ambiguous scheme of action,	81
His diplomacy seems pacific,	83
He engages England in naval movements tending to provoke war,	83
The Bosphorus and the Dardanelles,	83
The Sultan's ancient right to control them,	84
Policy of Russia in regard to the Straits,	85
The rights of the Sultan and the five Powers under the Treaty of 1841,	85
How those rights were affected by the Czar's seizure of the Principalities,	85
Powerful means of coercing the Czar,	86
Importance of refraining from a premature use of the power,	86
Naval movements in which the French Emperor engages England,	87

	Page
Proofs of this,	87
Means well fitted for enforcing a just peace so used to provoke war,	89

CHAPTER XVII.

Lord Stratford's scheme of pacification,	90
The "Vienna Note,"	91
Agreed to by the four Powers and accepted by Russia,	92
The French Emperor does nothing to thwart the success of the Note,	92
Lord Stratford had not been consulted,	93
The "Vienna Note" in the hands of Lord Stratford,	95
The Turkish Government determines to reject it unless altered,	97
Lord Stratford and the Turks stand alone in Europe,	97
They are firm,	97
Language used by Nesselrode,	98
The Protectorate of the Greek Church in Turkey still the thing in question,	98
The Porte declares war,	96
Warlike spirit of the belligerents,	99
Warlike ardour of the people in the Ottoman Empire,	99
Moderation of the Turkish Government,	100
Its effect on the mind of the Czar,	101
The Czar's proclamation,	101

CHAPTER XVIII.

Announcement by the Czar,	103
The negotiations are continued,	103
Movement at Constantinople,	104
The use made of this by the Turkish Ministers,	104
They succeed in alarming the French Ambassador,	105
Composure of Lord Stratford,	106
His wise and guarded measures,	106
The French Emperor. His means of putting a pressure upon the English Cabinet,	107

	Page
Violent urgency of the French Emperor for an advance of the fleets to Constantinople,	109
Needlessness of the measure,	109
Its tendency to bring on war,	110
The English Government yields to the French Emperor,	111
Fleet ordered up to Constantinople,	111
Want of firmness and discretion evinced in the adoption of the measure,	111
Baron Brunnow's remonstrance,	112
Effect of the measure at St Petersburg,	112
Count Nesselrode's sorrow,	112
The Czar's determination to retaliate,	114
Error of the notions regarding the disaster of Sinope,	114
Ostentatious publicity of the Russian operations in the Black Sea,	115
Tidings of an impending attack by the Russian fleet,	115
Inaction of the Ambassadors and the Admirals,	117
The disaster of Sinope,	119

CHAPTER XII.

Chasm in the instructions to the Admirals of the Western Powers,	121
Tends to bring blame upon the Home Government,	122
Reception of the tidings of Sinope in France and England,	122
The anger of the English people diverted towards the Czar,	122
An unjust charge against him gains belief in England,	123
First decision of the English Cabinet in regard to Sinope,	124
Lord Palmerston resigns office,	125
Proposal of the French Emperor,	125
Danger of breaking down the old barriers between peace and war,	125
Ambiguous character of the proposal,	126
The French Emperor presses upon the English Cabinet,	127
Lord Aberdeen's Cabinet yields,	128
Lord Palmerston withdraws his resignation,	129
Orders to execute the scheme and to announce it at St Petersburg,	132

CHAPTER XX.

	Page
Terms of settlement agreed to by the four Powers and forced upon the Turks,	131
Grounds for expecting an amicable solution,	132
Friendly reception by the Russian Government of the news of the first decision of the English Cabinet,	132
Announcement at St Petersburg of the scheme finally adopted by the Western Powers,	133
The negotiations are ruined,	134
Rupture of the diplomatic relations,	134
The Czar prepares to invade Turkey, and fleets enter the Euxine,	135

CHAPTER XXI.

Military error of the Czar in occupying Wallachia,	136
Of this Omar Pasha takes skilful advantage,	136
His autumn and winter campaigns,	137
Embarrassment and distress of the Czar,	138
He resorts for aid to Paskievitch,	139
Paskievitch's counsels,	140
Movement of troops in the Russian Empire,	142

CHAPTER XXII.

Sir John Burgoyne and Colonel Ardent despatched to the Levant,	143
Troops sent to Malta,	144
Tendency of this measure,	144
Ministers determine to propose but a small increase of the army,	145
Continuance of Lord Aberdeen's imprudent language,	145

CHAPTER XXIII.

The French Emperor's letter to the Czar,	147
Mission to St Petersburg from the English Peace Party,	150

CHAPTER XXIV.

	Page
Temper of the English an obstacle to the maintenance of peace,	152
Their desire for war,	153
Causes of the apparent change in their feeling,	153
State of feeling in the spring of 1853	156
Effect of the Czar's aggression upon the public mind,	158
Still in foreign affairs the nation looks for guidance to public men.	159
Lord Aberdeen,	159
Mr Gladstone,	161
Lord Aberdeen and Mr Gladstone remain in office,	163
Effect of this on the efforts of those who wished to prevent war,	163
The ruin of their cause not for want of grounds to stand upon,	165
Nor of oratorical power,	166
Mr Cobden and Mr Bright,	166
Reasons why they were able to make no stand,	167

CHAPTER XXV.

Meeting of Parliament,	171
The Queen's Speech,	172
The policy which it indicated,	174
The separate understanding with France,	174
Unswerving resolve of Austria and Prussia to rid the Principalities of Russian troops,	174
Proofs of this from transactions anterior to the Queen's Speech,	175
From transactions subsequent thereto,	178
The interests of Austria and Prussia begin to divide them from the Western Powers,	186
Austria and Prussia never swerve from their resolve,	187

CHAPTER XXVI.

Spirit of warlike adventure in England,	189
Its bearing upon the policy of the Government,	190
England's engagements with the French Emperor,	191

CONTENTS OF VOLUME II.

	Page
Into this policy the bulk of the Cabinet drift,	192
The Minister who went his own way,	192
Lord Palmerston's way of masking the tendency of the Government,	203
Debates upon the Address,	204
Parliament in the dark as to the real tendency of the Government,	204
Production of the papers,	206
Their effect,	206
Question on which the judgment of Parliament should have been rested,	207

CHAPTER XXVII.

Last step, which brought on the final rupture,	209
Austria's proposition,	210
Importance of avoiding haste,	211
Pressure of the French Emperor,	211
Eagerness of the people in England,	211
The Government loses its composure,	212
The summons despatched by England,	212
Instructions to the messenger,	213
And to Lord Westmorland,	213
Austria not required to take part in the summons,	213
The counter proposals of Russia reach Vienna,	214
They are rejected by the Conference of the four Powers	214
Austria and Prussia support the summons without taking part in the step,	215
The French summons,	215
France and England brought into a state of war with Russia,	215
Message from the French Emperor to the Chambers,	215
Message from the Queen to Parliament,	217
Declaration of war,	217
Difficulty of framing it,	218
The Czar's Declaration and War Manifesto,	218
His invasion of Turkey is commenced,	219
Treaty between the Sultan and the Western Powers,	220
Treaty between France and England,	220

CHAPTER XXVIII.

	Page
Recapitulation,	217
Standing causes of the disturbance,	222
Effect of personal government by the Czar,	222
By the Emperor of Austria,	223
By the King of Prussia,	224
By the French Emperor,	224
Share of Russia in bringing about the War,	225
Share of Turkey in causing it,	229
Share which Austria had,	231
In other respects Austria discharged her duty,	233
Share which Prussia had,	234
In other respects Prussia discharged her duty,	236
As did also the German Confederation,	237
Share which the French Government had in causing the war,	237
Share which England had,	240
The volitions which governed events,	247

APPENDIX.

	Page
Part I. — Papers showing the difference which led to the rupture of Prince Mentschikoff's negotiation,	251
Part II. — The "Vienna Note," with the proposed Turkish modifications, ...	256
Part III. — Papers showing the concord existing between the four Powers at the time when France and England were engaging in a separate course of action, ...	259
Part IV. — Note to page 43, ...	270

ILLUSTRATION TO VOL. II.

Plate I. . . . . to face page 136

INVASION OF THE CRIMEA.

CHAPTER XIV.

(CONTINUED.)

According to some, a shot was fired from a window or a house-top near the Rue du Sentier. This is denied by others, and one witness declares that the first shot came from a soldier near the centre of one of the battalions, who fired straight up into the air; but what followed was this: the troops at the head of the column faced about to the south and opened fire. Some of the soldiery fired point-blank into the mass of spectators who stood gazing upon them from the foot-pavement, and the rest of the troops fired up at the gay crowded windows and balconies.* The officers in general did not order the firing, but seemingly they were agitated in the same way as the men of the rank and file, for such of them as could be seen from a balcony at the corner of the Rue

---

* Captain Jesse, *ubi post*.

Montmartre appeared to acquiesce in all that the soldiery did.*

The impulse which had thus come upon the soldiery near the head of the column was a motive akin to panic, for it was carried by swift contagion from man to man till it ran westward from the Boulevard Bonne Nouvelle into the Boulevard Poissonière, and gained the Boulevard Montmartre, and ran swiftly through its whole length, and entered the Boulevard des Italiens. Thus by a movement in the nature of that which tacticians describe as "conversion," a column of some sixteen thousand men facing eastward towards St Denis was suddenly formed, as it were, into an order of battle fronting southward, and busily firing into the crowd which lined the footpavement, and upon the men, women, and children who stood at the balconies and windows on that side of the Boulevard.** What made the fire at the houses the more deadly was that, even after it had begun at the eastern part of the Boulevard Montmartre, people standing at the balconies and windows farther west could not see or believe that the troops were really firing in at the windows with ball-cartridge, and they remained in the front-rooms, and even continued standing at the windows, until a volley came crashing in. At one of the windows there stood a young Russian noble with his sister at his side.

* Captain Jesse, *ubi post*.
** Ibid.

Suddenly they received the fire of the soldiery, and both of them were wounded with musket-shots. An English surgeon, who had been gazing from another window in the same house, had the fortune to stand unscathed; and when he began to give his care to the wounded brother and sister, he was so touched, he says, by their forgetfulness of self, and the love they seemed to bear the one for the other, that more than ever before in all his life he prized his power of warding off death.

Of the people on the foot-pavement who were not struck down at first, some rushed and strove to find a shelter, or even a half-shelter, at any spot within reach. Others tried to crawl away on their hands and knees; for they hoped that perhaps the balls might fly over them. The impulse to shoot people had been sudden, but was not momentary. The soldiers loaded and reloaded with a strange industry, and made haste to kill and kill, as though their lives depended upon the quantity of the slaughter they could get through in some given period of time.

When there was no longer a crowd to fire into, the soldiers would aim carefully at any single fugitive who was trying to effect his escape, and if a man tried to save himself by coming close up to the troops, and asking for mercy, the soldiers would force or persuade the suppliant to keep off, and hasten away, and then, if they could, they killed him running. This slaughter of unarmed men and women was continued for a quarter of an hour or twenty minutes.

CHAP.
XIV.
It chanced that amongst the persons standing at the balconies near the corner of the Rue Montmartre there was an English officer; and because of the position in which he stood, the professional knowledge which guided his observation, the composure with which he was able to see and to describe, and the more than common responsibility which attaches upon a military narrator, it is probable that his testimony will be always appealed to by historians who shall seek to give a truthful account of the founding of the Second French Empire.

At the moment when the firing began, this officer was looking upon the military display with his wife at his side; and was so placed that if he looked eastward he could carry his eye along the Boulevard for a distance of about 800 yards, and see as far as the head of the column; and if he looked westward he could see to the point where the Boulevard Montmartre runs into the Boulevard des Italiens. This is what he writes: "I went to the balcony "at which my wife was standing, and remained there "watching the troops. The whole Boulevard, as far "as the eye could reach, was crowded with them, "— principally infantry in subdivisions at quarter "distance, with here and there a batch of twelve- "pounders and howitzers, some of which occupied "the rising ground of the Boulevard Poissonière. "The officers were smoking their cigars. The win- "dows were crowded with people, principally women, "tradesmen, servants, and children, or, like ourselves,

"the occupants of apartments. Suddenly, as I was
"intently looking with my glass at the troops in
"the distance eastward, a few musket-shots were
"fired at the head of the column, which consisted
"of about 3000 men. In a few moments it spread;
"and, after hanging a little, came down the Boulevard
"in a waving sheet of flame. So regular, however,
"was the fire that at first I thought it was a feu de
"joie for some barricade taken in advance, or to signal
"their position to some other division; and it was
"not till it came within fifty yards of me, that I re-
"cognised the sharp ringing report of ball-cartridge;
"but even then I could scarcely believe the evidence
"of my ears, for, as to my eyes, I could not discover
"any enemy to fire at; and I continued looking at
"the men until the company below me were actually
"raising their firelocks, and one vagabond sharper
"than the rest — a mere lad without whisker or mous-
"tache — had covered me. In an instant I dashed my
"wife, who had just stepped back, against the pier
"between the windows, when a shot struck the ceil-
"ing immediately over our heads, and covered us
"with dust and broken plaster. In a second after, I
"placed her upon the floor; and in another, a volley
"came against the whole front of the house, the
"balcony, and windows; one shot broke the mirror
"over the chimney-piece, another the shade of the
"clock; every pane of glass but one was smashed;
"the curtains and window-frames cut; the room, in
"short, was riddled. The iron balcony, though rather

"low, was a great protection; still fire-balls entered
"the room, and in the pause for reloading I drew my
"wife to the door, and took refuge in the back-rooms
"of the house. The rattle of musketry was incessant
"for more than a quarter of an hour after this; and
"in a very few minutes the guns were unlimbered
"and pointed at the 'Magasin' of M. Sallandrouze,
"five houses on our right. What the object or
"meaning of all this might be was a perfect enigma
"to every individual in the house, French or for-
"eigners. Some thought the troops had turned round
"and joined the Reds; others suggested that they
"must have been fired upon somewhere, though they
"certainly had not from our house or any other on
"the Boulevard Montmartre, or we must have seen
"it from the balcony. . . . This wanton fusilade must
"have been the result of a panic, lest the windows
"should have been lined with concealed enemies, and
"they wanted to secure their skins by the first fire, or
"else it was a sanguinary impulse. . . . The men, as
"I have already stated, fired volley upon volley for
"more than a quarter of an hour without any return;
"they shot down many of the unhappy individuals
"who remained on the Boulevard and could not ob-
"tain an entrance into any house; some persons were
"killed close to our door."* The like of what was
calmly seen by this English officer, was seen with

* Letter from Captain Jesse, first printed in the "Times," 13th December 1851, and given also in the "Annual Register."

frenzied horror by thousands of Frenchmen and women.

If the officers in general abstained from ordering the slaughter, Colonel Rochefort did not follow their example. He was an officer in the Lancers, and he had already done execution with his horsemen amongst the chairs and the idlers in the neighbourhood of Tortoni's; but afterwards imagining a shot to have been fired from a part of the Boulevard occupied by infantry, he put himself at the head of a detachment which made a charge upon the crowd; and the military historian of these events relates with triumph that about thirty corpses, almost all of them in the clothes of gentlemen, were the trophies of this exploit.* Along a distance of a thousand yards, going eastward from the Rue Richelieu, the dead bodies were strewed upon the foot-pavement of the Boulevard, but at several spots they lay in heaps. Some of the people mortally struck would be able to stagger blindly for a pace or two until they were tripped up by a corpse, and this, perhaps, is why a large proportion of the bodies lay heaped one on the other. Before one shop-front they counted thirty-three corpses. By the peaceful little nook or court which is called the Cité Bergère they counted thirty-seven.

---

* This was in the Boulevard Poissonière. Mauduit, p. 217, 218. Mauduit speaks of these thirty killed as armed men, but it is well proved that there were no armed men in the Boulevard Poissonière, and I have therefore no difficulty in rejecting that part of his statement.

CHAP. XIV.

The slayers were many thousands of armed soldiery: the slain were of a number that never will be reckoned; but amongst all these slayers and all these slain there was not one combatant. There was no fight, no riot, no fray, no quarrel, no dispute.* What happened was a slaughter of unarmed men, and women, and children. Where they lay, the dead bore witness. Corpses lying apart struck deeper into people's memory than the dead who were lying in heaps. Some were haunted with the look of an old man with silver hair, whose only weapon was the umbrella which lay at his side. Some shuddered because of seeing the gay idler of the Boulevard sitting dead against the wall of a house, and scarce parted from the cigar which lay on the ground near his hand. Some carried in their minds the sight of a printer's boy leaning back against a shop-front, because, though the lad was killed, the proof-sheets which he was carrying had remained in his hands, and were red with his blood, and were fluttering in the wind.** The military historian of these achievements permitted himself to speak with a kind of joy of the number of women who suffered. After accusing the gentler

---

* I speak here of the Boulevard from the Rue du Sentier to the western extremity of the Boulevard Montmartre.

** For accounts of the state of the Boulevard after the massacre, see the written statements of eyewitnesses supplied to Victor Hugo, and printed in his narrative. It will be seen that I do not adopt M. Victor Hugo's conclusions; but there is no reason for questioning the authenticity or the truth of the statements which he has collected.

sex of the crime of sheltering men from the fire of the troops, the Colonel writes it down that "many "an Amazon of the Boulevard has paid dearly for "her imprudent collusion with that new sort of bar-"ricade;" and then he goes on to express a hope that women will profit by the example and derive from it "a lesson for the future."* One woman who fell and died clasping her child, was suffered to keep her hold in death as in life, for the child too was killed. Words which long had been used for making figures of speech, recovered their ancient use, being wanted again in the world for the picturing of things real and physical. Musket-shots do not shed much blood in proportion to the slaughter which they work; but still in so many places the foot-pavement was wet and red, that, except by care, no one could pass along it without gathering blood. Round each of the trees in the Boulevards a little space of earth is left unpaved in order to give room for the expansion of the trunk. The blood collecting in pools upon the asphalte, drained down at last into these hollows, and there becoming coagulated, it remained for more than a day, and was observed by many. "Their blood,"— says the English officer before quoted, — "their "blood lay in the hollows round the trees the next "morning when we passed at twelve o'clock." "The "Boulevards and the adjacent streets," he goes on to say, "were at some points a perfect shambles."**

* Maudult, p. 279.
** Ibid., p. 279.

CHAP. XIV. Incredible as it may seem, artillery was brought to bear upon some of the houses in the Boulevard. On its north side the houses were so battered that the foot-pavement beneath them was laden with plaster and such ruins as field-guns can bring down.

The soldiers broke into many houses and hunted the inmates from floor to floor, and caught them at last and slaughtered them. These things, no doubt, they did under a notion that shots had been fired from the house which they entered; but it is certain that in almost all these instances, if not in every one of them, the impression was false. One or two soldiers would be seen rushing furiously at some particular door, and this sight leading their comrades to imagine that a shot had been fired from the windows above, was enough to bring into the accused house a whole band of slaughterers. The Sallandrouze carpet warehouse was thus entered. Fourteen helpless people shrank for safety behind some piles of carpets. The soldiers killed them crouching.

Slaughter in central Paris.

Whilst these things were being done upon the Boulevard, four brigades were converging upon the streets where resistance, though of a rash and feeble kind, had been really attempted. One after another the barricades were battered by artillery, and then carried without a serious struggle; but things had been so ordered that, although there should be little or no fighting, there might still be slaughter, for the converging movement of the troops prevented escape, and forced the people sooner or later into a street barred by troops on either side, and then, whether they were combatants or other fugitives, they were shot down. It was the success of this contrivance for penning in the fugitive crowds, which enabled Magnan to declare, without qualifying his words, that those who defended the barricades in the quartier Beaubourg were put to death;[*] and the same ground justified the Government in announcing that of the men who defended the barricade of the Porte St Martin the troops had not spared one.[**] Some of the people thus killed were men combating or flying, but many more were defenceless prisoners in the hands of the soldiery who shot them. Whatever may have been the cause of the slaughter of the unoffending spectators on the Boulevard,[***] it is certain that the shooting of the prisoners taken at the barricades was brought about by causing the troops to understand that they were to give no quarter. Over and over again, no doubt, the soldiers, listening to the dictates of humanity, gave quarter to vanquished combatants; but their clemency was looked upon as a fault, and the fault was repaired by shooting the prisoners they had taken. Sometimes, as was natural, a house was opened to the fugitives, but this shelter did not long hold good. For instance, when the barricade near the Porte St Denis

Slaughter of prisoners.

---

[*] See his Despatch dated, I think, the 9th December — "Moniteur."
[**] The "Patrie," one of the official organs of the President, Dec. 6.
[***] See the discussion on this subject towards the close of the chapter.

was taken, a hundred men were caught behind it, and all these were shot; but their blood was not reckoned to be enough; for, by going into the houses where there were supposed to be fugitives, the soldiers got hold of thirty more men, and these also they killed.* The way in which the soldiery dealt with the inmates of houses suspected of containing fugitives, can be gathered by observing what passed in one little street. After describing the capture of a barricade in the Rue Montorgueil, the military historian of these events says that searches were immediately ordered to be made in the public-houses. "A hundred prisoners," he says, "were made in "them, the most of whom had their hands still black "with gunpowder—an evident proof of their partici- "pation in the contest. How, then, was it possible "not to execute, with regard to a good many of "them, the terrible prescriptions of the state of "siege?"**

This killing was done under orders so stringent, and yet, in some instances, with so much of deliberation, that many of the poor fellows put to death were allowed to dispose of their little treasures before they died. Thus, one man, when told that he must die, entreated the officer in command to be allowed to send to his mother the fifteen francs which he

---

* An officer engaged in the operation made this statement — not as a confession of sins, but as a narrative of exploits.

** Mauduit, p. 248.

carried in his pocket. The officer, consenting, took down the address of the man's mother, received from him the fifteen francs, and then killed him. Many times over the like of this was done.

Great numbers of prisoners were brought into the Prefecture of Police, but it appears to have been thought inconvenient to allow the sound of the discharge of musketry to be heard coming from the precincts of the building. For that reason, as it would seem, another mode of quieting men was adopted. It is hard to have to believe such things, but according to the statement of a former member of the Legislative Assembly, who declares that he saw them with his own eyes, each of the prisoners destined to undergo this fate was driven, with his hands tied behind him, into one of the courts of the Prefecture, and then one of Maupas's police-officers came and knocked him on the head with a loaded club, and felled him—felled him in the way that is used by a man when he has to slaughter a bullock.*

Troops are sometimes obliged to kill insurgents

---

* M. Xavier Durrieu, formerly a member of the Assembly, is one of those who states that he was an eyewitness of these deeds, having seen them from the window of his cell. He says, "Souvent quand la "porte était renfermée les sergens de ville se jetaient comme des tigres "sur les prisonniers attachés les mains derrière le dos. Ils les assom-"maient à coup de casse-tête. Ils les laissaient râlant sur la pierre où "plusieurs d'entre eux ont expiré. . . . Il en est ainsi ni plus ni "moins; nous l'avons vu des fenêtres de nos cellules qui s'ouvraient "sur la cour." — *Le Coup d'État*, par Xavier Durrieu, ancien Représentant du peuple, pp. 39, 40.

CHAP. XIV.

Gradations by which slayers of vanquished men may be distinguished.

in actual fight, and unarmed people standing in the line of fire often share the fate of the combatants; what that is the whole world understands. But also an officer has sometimes caused people to be put to death, not because they were fighting against him, nor even because they were hindering the actual operations of the troops, but because he has imagined that under some probable change of circumstance their continued presence might become a source of inconvenience or danger, and he has therefore thought it right to have them shot down by way of precaution; but generally such an act as this has been preceded by the most earnest entreaties to disperse, and by repeated warnings. This may be called a precautionary slaughter of bystanders, who are foolhardy or perverse, or wilfully obstructive to the troops. Again, it has happened that a slaughter of this last-mentioned sort has occurred, but without having been preceded by any such request or warning as would give the people time to disperse. This is a wilful and malignant slaughter of bystanders; but still it is a slaughter of bystanders whose presence might become inconvenient to the troops, and therefore, perhaps, it is not simply wanton. Again, it has happened (as we have but too well seen) that soldiers not engaged in combat, and exposed to no real danger, have suddenly fired into the midst of crowds of men and women who neither opposed nor obstructed them. This is "wanton massacre." Again, it has sometimes happened, even in modern times, that when men defeated in fight have thrown down their arms and surrendered themselves, asking for mercy, the soldiery to whom they appealed have refused their prayers, and have instantly killed them. This is called "giving no quarter." Again, it has happened that defeated combatants, having thrown down their arms and surrendered at discretion, and not having been immediately killed, have succeeded in constituting themselves the prisoners of the vanquishing soldiery, but presently afterwards (as, for instance, within the time needed for taking the pleasure of an officer on horseback at only a few yards' distance) they have been put to death. This is called "killing prisoners." Again, defeated combatants, who have succeeded in constituting themselves prisoners, have been allowed to remain alive for a considerable time, and have afterwards been put to death by their captors with circumstances indicating deliberation. This is called "killing prisoners "in cold blood." Again, soldiers after a fight in a city have rushed into houses where they believed that there were people who helped or favoured their adversaries, and, yielding to their fury, have put to death men and women whom they had never seen in combat against them. This is massacre of non-combatants, but it is massacre committed by men still hot from the fight. Again, it has happened that soldiery, seizing unarmed people whom they believed to be favourers of their adversaries, have nevertheless checked their fury, and, instead of killing them,

CHAP. XIV.

Slaughter ranging under all those categories was caused by the confederates.

have made them prisoners; but afterwards, upon the arrival of orders from men more cruel than the angry soldiery, these people have been put to death. This is called an "execution of non-combatants in cold "blood."

Here, then, are acts of slaughter of no less than nine kinds, and of nine kinds so distinct that they do not merely differ in their accidents, but are divided, the one from the other, by strong moral gradations. It is certain that deeds ranging under all these nine categories were done in Paris on the 4th of December 1851, and it is not less certain that, although they were not all of them specifically ordered, they were, every one of them, caused by the brethren of the Elysée. Moreover, it must be remembered that this slaughtering of prisoners was the slaughtering of men against whom it was only to be charged that they were in arms, not to violate, but to defend the laws of their country.

Inquiry as to the alleged shooting of prisoners who were in the hands of the civil power.

But there is yet another use to which, if it were not for the honest pride of its officers and men, it would be possible for an army to be put. In the course of an insurrection in such a city as Paris, numbers of prisoners might be seized either by the immense police force which would probably be hard at its work, or by troops who might shrink from the hatefulness of refusing quarter to men without arms in their hands; and the prisoners thus taken, being consigned to the ordinary jails, would be in the custody of the civil power. The Government, regretting that many of the prisoners should have been taken alive, might perhaps desire to put them to death, but might be of opinion that it would be impolitic to kill them by the hand of the civil power. In this strait, if it were not for the obstacle likely to be interposed by the honour and just pride of a warlike profession, platoons of foot-soldiers might be used — not to defend — not to attack — not to fight, but to relieve the civilians from one of the duties which they are accustomed to deem most vile, by performing for them the office of the executioner; and these platoons might even be ordered to help the Government to hide the deed by doing their work in the dead hours of the night.

Is it true that, with the sanction of the Home Office and of the Prefecture of Police, and under the orders of Prince Louis Bonaparte, St Arnaud, Magnan, Morny, and Maupas, a midnight work of this last kind was done by the army of Paris?

To men not living in the French capital, it seems that there is a want of complete certainty about the fate of a great many out of those throngs of prisoners who were brought into the jails and other places of detention on the 4th and 5th of December. The people of Paris think otherwise. They seem to have no doubt. The grounds of their belief are partly of this sort: — A family, anxious to know what had become of one of their relatives who was missing, appealed for help to a man in so high a station of life that they deemed him powerful enough to be able to question official personages, and his is the

CHAP. XIV.

testimony which records what passed. In order, if possible, to find a clue to the fate of the lost man, he made the acquaintance of one of the functionaries who held the office of a "Judge-Substitute." The moment the subject of inquiry was touched, the "Judge-Substitute" began to boil with anger at the mere thought of what he had witnessed, but it seems that his indignation was not altogether unconnected with offended pride, and the agony of having had his jurisdiction invaded. He said that he had been ordered to go to some of the jails and examine the prisoners, with a view to determine whether they should be detained or set free; and that, whilst he was engaged in this duty, a party of non-commissioned officers and soldiers came into the room and rudely announced that they themselves had orders to dispose of those prisoners whose fingers were black. Then, without regard to the protesting of the "Judge-Substitute," they examined the hands of the prisoners whom he had before him, adjudged that the fingers of many of them were black, and at once carried off all those whom they so condemned, with a view (as the "Judge-Substitute" understood) to shoot them, or have them shot. That they were so shot the "Judge-Substitute" was certain, but it is plain that he had no personal knowledge of what was done to the prisoners after they were carried off by the soldiers. Again, during the night of the 4th and the night of the 5th, people listening in one of the undisturbed quarters of Paris would suddenly hear the volley of a single platoon — a sound not heard, they say, at such hours either before or since. The sound of this occasional platoon-firing was heard coming chiefly, it seems, from the Champ de Mars, but also from other spots, and, in particular, from the gardens of the Luxembourg, and from the esplanade of the Invalides. People listening within hearing of this last spot declared, they say, that the sound of the platoon-fire was followed by shrieks and moans; and that once, in the midst of the other cries, they caught some piteous words, close followed by a scream, and sounding as though they were the words of a lad imperfectly shot and dying hard.

Partly upon grounds of this sort, but more perhaps by the teaching of universal fame, Paris came to believe—and, rightly or wrongly, Paris still believes—that during the night of the 4th, and again during the night of the 5th, prisoners were shot in batches and thrown into pits. On the other hand, the adherents of the French Emperor deny that the troops did duty as executioners.* Therefore the value of an Imperialist denial, with all such weight as may be thought to belong to it, is set against the imperfect proof on which Paris founds her belief; but men must remember why it is that any obscurity can hang upon a question like this. The question whether, on the night of a given Thursday and a given Friday,

* Granier de Cassaignac, vol. ii.

CHAP. XIV. whole batches of men living in Paris were taken out and shot by platoons in such places as the Champ de Mars or the Luxembourg gardens—this is a question which, from its very nature, could not have remained in doubt for forty-eight hours, unless Paris at the time had lost her freedom of speech and her freedom of printing; and even now, after a lapse of years, if freedom were restored to France, the question would be quickly and righteously determined. Now it happens that those who took away from Paris her freedom of speech and her freedom of printing are the very persons of whom it is said that during two December nights they caused their fellow-countrymen to be shot by platoons and in batches. So it comes to this, that those who are charged have made away with the means by which the truth might be best established. In this stress, Justice is not so dull and helpless as to submit to be baffled. Wisely deviating in such a case from her common path, she listens for a moment to incomplete testimony against the concealer, and then, by requiring that he who hid away the truth shall restore it to light, or abide the consequence of his default, she shifts the duty of giving strict proof from the accuser to the accused. Because Prince Louis and his associates closed up the accustomed approaches to truth, therefore it is cast upon them either to remain under the charge which Paris brings against them, or else to labour and show, as best they may, that they did not cause batches of

French citizens to be shot by platoons of infantry in the night of the 4th and the night of the 5th of December.

<small>CHAP. XIV.</small>

The whole number of people killed by the troops during the forty hours which followed upon the commencement of the massacre in the Boulevards, will never be known. The burying of the bodies was done for the most part at night. In searching for a proximate notion of the extent of the carnage, it is not safe to rely even upon the acknowledgments of the officers engaged in the work, for during some time they were under an impression that it was favourable to a man's advancement to be supposed to be much steeped in what was done. The colonel of one of the regiments engaged in this slaughter spoke whilst the business was fresh in his mind. It would be unsafe to accept his statement as accurate, or even as substantially true; but as it is certain that the man had taken part in the transactions of which he spoke, and that he really wished to gain credence for the words which he uttered, his testimony has a kind of value as representing (to say the least of it) his idea of what could be put forward as a credible statement by one who had the means of knowing the truth. What he declared was that his regiment alone had killed two thousand four hundred men. Supposing that his statement was anything like an approach to the truth, and that his corps was at all rivalled by others, a very high number would be

<small>Uncertainty as to the number of people killed.</small>

CHAP. XIV.

Total loss of the army in killed.

Effect of the massacre upon the people of Paris.

wanted for recording the whole quantity of the slaughter.*

In the army which did these things, the whole number of killed was twenty-five.**

Of all men dwelling in cities the people of Paris are perhaps the most warlike. Less almost than any other Europeans are they accustomed to overvalue the lives of themselves and their fellow-citizens. With them the joy of the fight has power to overcome fear and grief, and they had been used to great street-battles; but they had not been used of late to witness the slaughter of people unarmed and helpless. At the sight of what was done on that 4th of December the great city was struck down as though by a plague. A keen-eyed Englishman, who chanced to come upon some of the people retreating from these scenes of slaughter, declared that their countenances were of a strange livid hue which he had never before seen. This was because he had never before seen the faces of men coming straight from the witnessing of a massacre. They say that the shock of being within sight and hearing the shrieks broke down the nervous strength of many a brave though tender man, and

---

* The number of regiments operating against Paris was between thirty and forty, and of these about twenty belonged to the divisions which were actively employed in the work.

** Including all officers and soldiers killed from the 3d to the 6th of December. The official return, "Moniteur," p. 3062.

caused him to burst into sobs as though he were a little child.

Before the morning of the 5th the armed insurrection had ceased. From the first it had been feeble. On the other hand, the moral resistance which was opposed to the acts of the President and his associates had been growing in strength; and when the massacre began on the afternoon of the 4th of December, the power of this moral resistance was in the highest degree formidable. Yet it came to pass that, by reason of the strange prostration of mind which was wrought by the massacre, the armed insurrection dragged down with it in its fall the whole policy of those who conceived that by the mere force of opinion and ridicule they would be enabled to send the plotters to Vincennes. The Cause of those who intended to rely upon this scheme of moral resistance, was in no way mixed up with the attempts of the men of the barricades, but still it was a Cause which depended upon the high spirit of the people; and it had happened that this spirit — perplexed and baffled on the 2d of December by a stratagem and a night attack — was now crushed out by sheer horror.

For her beauty, for her grandeur, for her historic fame, for her warlike deeds, for her power to lead the will of a mighty nation, and to crown or discrown its monarchs, no city on earth is worthy to be the rival of Paris. Yet, because of the palsy that came upon her after the slaughter on the Boulevard, this Paris — this beauteous, heroic Paris — this queen

CHAP. XIV.

of great renown, was delivered bound into the hands of Prince Louis Bonaparte, and Morny, and Maupas or De Maupas, and St Arnaud formerly Le Roy. And the benefit which Prince Louis derived from the massacre was not transitory. It is a maxim of French politics that, happen what may, a man seeking to be a ruler of France must not be ridiculous. From 1836 until 1848 Prince Louis had never ceased to be obscure except by bringing upon himself the laughter of the world; and his election into the chair of the Presidency had only served to bring upon him a more constant outpouring of the scorn and sarcasm which Paris knows how to bestow.* Even the suddenness and perfect success of the blow struck in the night between the 1st and the 2d of December had failed to make Paris think of him with gravity. But it was otherwise after three o'clock on the 4th of December; and it happened that the most strenuous adversaries of this oddly fated Prince were those who, in one respect, best served his cause; for the more they strove to show that he, and he alone, of his own design and malice had planned and ordered the massacre,** the more completely they relieved him from the disqualification which had hitherto made it im-

Effect of the massacre in removing one of Louis Bonaparte's personal disqualifications.

---

* A glance at the "Charivari" for '49, '50, and the first eleven months of '51, would verify this statement. The stopping of the "Charivari" was one of the very first exertions of the supreme power which was seized in the night of the 2d of December.

** It will be seen (see post) that I question the truth of this charge against him.

possible for him to become the supreme ruler of France. Before the night closed in on the 4th of December, he was sheltered safe from ridicule by the ghastly heaps on the Boulevard.

The fate of the provinces resembled the fate of the capital. Whilst it was still dark on the morning of the 2d, Morny, stealing into the Home Office, had intrusted his orders for instant and enthusiastic support to the zeal of every prefect, and had ordered that every mayor, every juge de paix, and every other public functionary who failed to give in his instant and written adhesion to the acts of the President, should be dismissed. In France the engine of State is so constructed as to give to the Home Office an almost irresistible power over the provinces, and the means which the Office had of coercing France were reinforced by an appeal to men's fears of anarchy, and their dread of the sect called "Socialists." Forty thousand communes were suddenly told that they must make swift choice between Socialism and anarchy and rapine on the one hand, and on the other a virtuous dictator and lawgiver, recommended and warranted by the authority of Monsieur de Morny. The gifted Montalembert himself was so effectually caught in this springe that he publicly represented the dilemma as giving no choice except between Louis Bonaparte and "the ruin of France." In the provinces, as in Paris, there were men whose love of right was stronger than their fears of the Executive Government, and stronger than their dread of the Socialists; but the Departments, being kept in utter darkness by the arrangements of the Home Office, were slower than Paris in finding out that the blow of the 2d of December had been struck by a small knot of associates, without the concurrence of Statesmen who were the friends of law and order; and it would seem that, although the proclamations were received at first with stupor and perplexity, they soon engendered a hope that the President (acting, as the country people imagined him to be, with the support of many eminent Statesmen) might effect a wholesome change in the Constitution, and restore to France some of the tranquillity and freedom which she had enjoyed under the Government of her last King. There were risings, but every department which seemed likely to move was put under martial law. Then followed slaughter, banishment, imprisonment, sequestration; and all this at the mere pleasure of Generals raging with a cruel hatred of the people, and glowing with the glow of that motive — so hateful because so sordid — which in centralised states men call "zeal." Of these Generals there were some who, in their fury, went beyond all the bounds of what could be dictated by anything like policy, even though of the most ferocious kind. In the department of the Allier, for instance, it was decreed, not only that all who were "known" to have taken up arms against the Government should be tried by Court-Martial, but that "those whose

"Socialist opinions were notorious" should be transported by the mere order of the Administration, and have their property sequestered. The bare mental act of holding a given opinion was thus put into the category of black crimes; and either the prisoner was to have no trial at all, or else he was to be tried, as it were, by the hangman. This decree was issued by a man called General Eynard, and was at once adopted and promulgated by the Executive Government.*

The violence with which the brethren of the Elysée were raging took its origin, no doubt, from their terror; but now that they were able to draw breath, another motive began to govern them, and to drive them along the same road: for by this time they were able to give to their actions a colour which tended to bring them the support and goodwill of whole multitudes — whole multitudes distracted with fear of the democrats, and only longing for safety. For more than three years people had lived in dread of the "Socialists;" and though the sect, taken alone, was never so formidable as to justify the alarm of a firm man, still it was more or less allied with the fierce species of democrat which men called "Red," and the institutions of the Republic being new and weak, it was right for the nation to stand on its guard against anarchy; though many have judged that the defenders of

---

* "Moniteur," 28th Dec.

order, being upheld by the voice of the millions no less than by the forces of intellect and of property, might have kept their watch without fear. But whether the thing from which people ran flying was a danger or only a phantom, the terror it spread brought numbers down into a state which was hardly other than abject. Of course, people thus unmanned would look up piteously to the Executive Government as their natural protectors, and would be willing to offer their freedom in exchange for a little more safety. So now, if not before, the company of the Elysée saw the gain which would accrue to them if they could have it believed that their enterprise was a war against Socialism. After the subjugation of Paris, the scanty gatherings of people who took up arms against the Government were composed, no doubt, partly of Socialists, but partly also of men who had no motive for rising, except that they were of too high a spirit to be able to stand idle and see the law trampled down. But the brotherhood of the Elysée was master — sole master — of the power to speak in print; and by exaggerating the disturbances going on in some parts of France, as well as by fastening upon all who stood up against them the name of the hated sect, they caused it to be believed by thousands, and perhaps by millions, that they were engaged in a valorous and desperate struggle against Socialism. In proportion as this pretence came to be believed, it brought hosts of people to the support of the Executive Government;

and there is reason to believe that, even among those of the upper classes who seemed to be standing proudly aloof from the Elysée, there were many who secretly rejoiced to be delivered from their fear of the Democrats at the price of having to see France handled for a time by persons like Morny and Maupas.

<small>CHAP. XIV.
Support thus obtained.</small>

The truth is, that in the success of this speculation of the Elysée many thought they saw how to escape from the vexations of democracy in a safe and indolent way. When an Arab decides that the burnous, which is his garment by day and by night, has become unduly populous, he lays it upon an ant-hill in order that the one kind of insect may be chased away by the other; and, as soon as this has been done, he easily brushes off the conquering genus with the stroke of a whip or a pipe-stick. In a lazy mood well-born men thought to do this with France; and the first part of the process was successful enough, for all the red sort were killed or crushed or hunted away; but when that was done, it began to appear that those whose hungry energies had been made use of to do the work were altogether unwilling to be brushed off. They clung: even now, after the lapse of years,* they cling and feed.

The army in the provinces closely imitated the ferocity of the army of Paris; but it was to be apprehended that soldiery, however fierce, might deal

<small>Commissaries sent into the provinces.</small>

---

* Written in September 1861.

only with the surface of discontent, and not strike deep enough into the heart of the country. They might kill people in streets and roads and fields; they might even send their musket-balls through windows into the houses, and shoot whole batches of prisoners; but they could not so well search out the indignant friends of law and order in their inner homes. Therefore Morny sent into the provinces men of dire repute, and armed them with terrible powers. These persons were called Commissaries. In every spot so visited the people shuddered; for they knew by their experience of 1848 that a man thus set over them by the terrible Home Office might be a ruffian well known to the police for his crimes as well as for his services, and that from a potentate of that quality it might cost them dear to buy their safety.

The Church.

There have been times when the all but dying spark of a nation's life has been kept alive by the priests of her faith; and when this has happened, there has sprung up so deep a love between people and Church that the lapse of ages has not had strength to put the two asunder.* In France, it is true, the Church no longer wielded the authority which had belonged to her of old; but besides that the virtues of her humble and labouring priesthood had gained for her more means of guiding men's minds than

---

* See Arthur Stanley's admirable account of the relations between Russia and her Church.

Europe was accustomed to believe, she was a cohering and organised body. Therefore, at a moment when the whole temporal powers of the State had been seized by a small knot of men slyly acting in concert, and when the Parliamentary and judicial authority which might restrain their violence had been all at once overthrown, the Church of France, surviving in the midst of ruined institutions, became suddenly invested with a great power to do good or do evil. She might stand between the armed man and his victim; she might turn away wrath; she might make conditions for prostrate France. Or, taking a yet loftier stand, she might resolve to choose — and choose sternly — between right and wrong. She chose.

The priesthood of France were, upon the whole, a zealous, unworldly, devoted body of men; but already the Church which they served had been gained over to the President by the arrangements which led to the siege and occupation of Rome. Therefore, although the priests perceived that Maupas, coming privily in the night-time, had seized the generals and the statesmen of France, and had shut up the Parliament, and driven the judges from the judgment-seat, still it seemed to them that, because of Rome, they ought to side with Maupas. So far as concerned her political action in this time of trial, they suffered the Church of France to degenerate into a mere sub-department of the Home Office. In the rural districts, when the time for the Plebiscite came, they

CHAP. XIV.

France disarmed.

fastened tickets marked "Yes" upon their people, and drove them in flocks to the poll.

Every institution in the country being thus suborned or enslaved, or shattered, the brethren of the Elysée resolved to follow up their victory over France. In the sense which will presently appear they resolved to disman her. It had resulted, from the political state of France during several years, that great numbers of the most stirring men in the country had belonged to clubs, which the law called "secret societies." A net thrown over this class would gather into its folds whole myriads of honest men; and indeed it has been computed that the number of persons then alive who at one time or other had belonged to some kind of "secret society," amounted to no less than two millions. If French citizens at some period of their lives had belonged to societies forbidden by Statute, it was enough (and, after a lapse of time, much more than enough) that the penalties of the law which they had disobeyed should be enforced against them. But it was not this, nor the like of this, that was done.

Prince Louis Bonaparte and Morny, with the advice and consent of Maupas, issued a retro-operative decree, by which all these hundreds of thousands of Frenchmen were made liable to be instantly seized, and transported either to the penal settlements in Africa, or to the torrid swamps of Cayenne.* The

---

* Decree of 8th December, inserted in the "Moniteur" of the 9th.

decree was as comprehensive as a law would be in England if it enacted that every man who had ever attended a political meeting might be now suddenly transported; but it was a hundred times less merciful; for, in general, to be banished to Cayenne was to be put to a slow, cruel, horrible death. Morny and Maupas pressed and pressed the execution of this almost incredible decree with a ferocity which must have sprung in the first instance from terror, and was afterwards kept alive for the sake of that hideous sort of popularity which was to be gained by calling men Socialists, and then fiercely hunting them down. None will ever know the number of men who at this period were either killed or imprisoned in France, or sent to die in Africa or Cayenne; but the panegyrist of Louis Bonaparte and his fellow-plotters acknowledges that the number of people who were seized and transported within the few weeks which followed the 2d of December, amounted to the enormous number of twenty-six thousand five hundred.*

France perhaps could have borne the loss of many tens of thousand of ordinary soldiers and workmen without being visibly weakened; but no nation in the world — no, not even France herself — is so abounding in the men who will dare something for honour and liberty, as to be able to bear to lose in one month between twenty and thirty thousand men, seized from out of her most stirring and most courageous citizens. It could not be but that what

CHAP. XIV.

26,500 men transported.

* Granier de Cassaignac.

CHAP. XIV. remained of France when she had thus been stricken should for years seem to languish and to be of a poor spirit. This is why I have chosen to say that France was dismanned.

But besides the men killed and the men transported, there were some thousands of Frenchmen who were made to undergo sufferings too horrible to be here told. I speak of those who were enclosed in the casemates of the fortresses and huddled down between the decks of the Canada and the Duguesclin. These hapless beings were, for the most part, men attached to the cause of the Republic. It would seem that of the two thousand men whose sufferings are the most known, a great part were men whose lives had been engaged in literary pursuits; for amongst them there were authors of some repute, editors of newspapers, and political writers of many grades, besides lawyers, physicians, and others whose labours in the field of politics had been mainly labours of the intellectual sort. The torments inflicted upon these men lasted from two to three months. It was not till the second week in March that a great many of them came out into the light and the pure air of Heaven. Because of what they had suffered they were hideous and terrible to look upon. The hospitals received many. It is right that the works which testify of these things should be indicated as authorities on which the narrator founds his passing words;[*]

[*] "Le Coup d'État," par Xavier Durrieu, ancien Représentant du Peuple. "Histoire de la Terreur Bonapartiste," par Hippolyte Magen.

but unless a man be under some special motive for learning the detailed truth, it would be well for him to close his eyes against those horrible pages; for if once he looks and reads, the recollection of the things he reads of may haunt him and weigh upon his spirit till he longs and longs in vain to recover his ignorance of what, even in this his own time, has been done to living men.

The Plebiscite.

At length the time came for the operation of what was called the Plebiscite. The arrangements of the plotters had been of such a kind as to allow France no hope of escape from anarchy and utter chaos, except by submitting herself to the dictatorship of Louis Bonaparte; for although the President in his Proclamation had declared that if the country did not like his Presidency they might choose some other in his place, no such alternative was really offered. The choice given to the electors did not even purport to be anything but a choice between Louis Bonaparte and nothing. According to the wording of the Plebiscite, a vote given for any candidate other than Louis Bonaparte would have been null. An elector was only permitted to vote "Yes," or vote "No;" and it seems plain that the prospect of anarchy involved in the negative vote would alone have operated as a sufficing menace. Therefore, even if the collection of the suffrages had been carried on with perfect fairness, the mere stress of the question proposed would have made it impossible that there should be a free election: the same central power

Causes rendering free election impossible.

which, nearly four years before, had compelled the terrified nation to pretend that it loved a republic, would have now forced the same helpless people to kneel, and say they chose for their one only lawgiver the man recommended to them by Monsieur de Morny.

Having the army and the whole executive power in their hands, and having preordained the question to be put to the people, the brethren of the Elysée, it would seem, might have safely allowed the proceeding to go to its sure conclusion without further coercing the vote; and if they had done thus, they would have given a colour to the assertion that the result of the Plebiscite was a national ratification of their act. But, remembering what they had done, and having blood on their hands, they did not venture upon a free election. What they did was this: they placed thirty-two departments under martial law; and since they wanted nothing more than a sheet of paper and a pen and ink in order to place every other department in the same predicament, it can be said without straining a word, that potentially, or actually, the whole of France was under martial law.

Therefore men voted under the sword. But martial law is only one of the circumstances which constitute the difference between an honest election and a Plebiscite of the Bonaparte sort. Of course, for all effective action on the part of multitudes, some degree of concert is needful; and on the side of the plotters, using as they did the resistless engine of the executive government, the concert was perfect.

To the adversaries of the Elysée all effective means of concerted action were forbidden by Morny and Maupas. Not only could they have no semblance of a public meeting, but they could not even venture upon the slightest approach to those lesser gatherings which are needed for men who want to act together. Of course, in these days, the chief engine for giving concerted and rational action to bodies of men is the Press. But, except for the uses of the Elysée, there was no Press. All journals hostile to the plot were silenced. Not a word could be printed which was unfavourable to Monsieur Morny's candidate for the dictatorship. Even the printing and distributing of negative voting-tickets was made penal; and during the ceremony which was called an "election," several persons were actually arrested, and charged with the offence of distributing negative voting-tickets, or persuading others to vote against the President. It was soon made clear that, so far as concerned his means of taking a real part in the election, every adversary of the Elysée was as helpless as a man deaf and dumb.

In one department it was decreed that any one spreading reports or suggesting fears tending to disquiet the people, should be instantly arrested and brought before a court-martial.* In another, every society, and indeed every kind of meeting, however

---

* Arrêté du Général d'Alphonse, Commandant l'état de siège dans le Département du Cher, Article 4.

CHAP. XIV. few the persons composing it might be, was in terms prohibited;* and it was announced that any man disobeying the order would be deemed to be a member of a secret society within the meaning of the terrible decree of the 8th of December, and liable to transportation.** In the same department it was decreed, that every one hawking or distributing printed tickets, or even manuscripts, unless authorised by the mayor or the juge de paix, should be prosecuted; and the same prefect, in almost mad rage against freedom, proclaimed that any one who was caught in an endeavour to "propagate an opinion" should be deemed guilty of exciting to civil war, and instantly handed over to the judicial authority.*** In another department the sub-prefect announced that any one who threw a doubt on the loyalty of the acts of the Government should be arrested.†

These are samples of the means which generals and prefects and sub-prefects adopted for insuring the result; but it is hardly to be believed that all this base zeal was really needed, because from the very first the brethren of the Elysée had taken a step which, even if it had stood alone, would have been more than enough to coerce the vote. They fixed for the 20th and 21st of December the election to which civilians were invited; but long before this

* Arrêté du Préfet de la Haute Garonne, Articles 1, 2, 9.
** Ibid. Article 3.
*** Ibid. Article 4.
† Arrêté du Sous-préfet de Valenciennes.

the army had been ordered to vote (and to vote openly without ballot), within forty-eight hours from the receipt of a despatch of the 3d of December. So all the land-forces of France had voted, as it were, by beat of drum, and the result of their voting had been made known to the whole country long before the time fixed for the civilians to proceed to election. France, therefore, if she were to dare to vote against the President, would be placing herself in instant and open conflict with the declared will of her own army, and this at a time when, to the extent already stated, she was under martial law.

CHAP. XIV.

Contrivance for coercing the election by the vote of the army.

Surprised, perplexed, affrighted, and all unarmed and helpless, France was called upon either to strive to levy a war of despair against the mighty engine of the French executive government, and the vast army which stood over her, or else to succumb at once to Louis Bonaparte and Morny and Maupas and Monsieur Le Roy St Arnaud. She succumbed. The brethren of the Elysée had asked the country to say "Yes" or "No:" should Louis Bonaparte alone build a new Constitution for the governance of the mighty nation? and when, in the way already told, they had obtained the "Yes" from herds and flocks of men whom they ventured to number at nearly eight millions, it was made known to Paris that the person who had long been the favourite subject of her jests was now become sole lawgiver for her and for France. In the making of such laws as he

France succumbed.

CHAP. XIV.

Prince Louis sole lawgiver of France.

intended to give the country, Prince Louis was highly skilled, for he knew how to enfold the creation of a sheer Oriental autocracy in a nomenclature taken from the polity of free European States. With the advice and consent of Morny, and no doubt with the full approval of all the rest of the plotters, he virtually made it the law that he should command, and that France should pay him tribute and obey.

The laws he gave her.

Importance of the massacre on the Boulevard.

It has been seen that the success of the plot of the 2d of December resulted from the massacre which took place in the Boulevard on the following Thursday; and since this strange event became the foundation of a momentous change in the polity of France, and even in the destinies of Europe, it is right for men to know, if they can, how and why it came to pass. At three o'clock on the afternoon of the 4th of December, the ultimate success of the plot had seemed to become almost hopeless by reason of the isolation to which Prince Louis and his associates were reduced. But at that hour the massacre began, and before the bodies were cleared away, the brethren of the Elysée had Paris and France at their mercy. It was natural that wronged and angry men, seeing this cause and this effect, should be capable of believing that the massacre was wilfully planned as a means of achieving the result which it actually produced. Just as the Cambridge theologian maintained that he who looked upon a watch must needs believe in a watchmaker, so men who had seen the massacre

Inquiry into its cause.

were led to infer a demon. They saw that the massacre brought wealth and blessings to the Elysée, and they thought it a safe induction to say that the man who gathered the harvest as though it were his own must have sown the seed in due season. Yet, so far as one knows, this argument from design is not very well reinforced by external proof; and perhaps it is more consistent with the principles of human nature to believe that the slaughter of the Boulevard resulted from the mixed causes which are known to have been in operation, than from a cold design on the part of the President to have a quantity of peaceful men and women killed in order that the mere horror of the sight might crush the spirit of Paris. Without resorting to this dreadful solution, the causes of the massacre may be reached by fair conjecture.

CHAP XIV.

The army, as we have seen, was burning with hatred of the civilians, and its ferocity had been carefully whetted by the President and by St Arnaud. This feeling, apart from other motives of action, would not have induced the brave soldiery of France to fire point-blank into crowds of defenceless men and women; but a passion more cogent than anger was working in the bosoms of the men at the Elysée and the Generals in command, and from them it descended to the troops.

According to its nature, and the circumstances in which it is placed, a creature struck by terror may

The passion of terror.

CHAP. XIV.
either lie trembling in a state of abject prostration, or else may be convulsed with hysteric energy; and when terror seizes upon man or beast in this last way, it is the fiercest and most blind of all passions. The French unite the delicate, nervous organisation of the south with much of the energy of the north; and they are keenly susceptible of the terror that makes a man kill people, and the terror that makes him lie down and beg. On that 4th of December, Paris was visited with terror in either form. The army raged and the people crouched; but army and people alike were governed by terror. It is very true that in the Boulevard there were no physical dangers which could have struck the troops with this truculent sort of panic; for even if it is believed that two or three shots were fired from a window or a housetop, an occurrence of that kind, in a quarter which was plainly prepared for sight-seeing and not for strife, was too trivial of itself to be capable of disturbing prime troops. But the President and his associates, though they had succeeded in all their mechanical arrangements, had failed to obtain the support of men of character and eminence. For that reason they were obviously in peril; and if Morny and Fleury still remained in good heart, there is no reason for doubting that on the 4th of December the sensations of the President, of the two other Bonapartes, of Maupas, of St Arnaud, and of Magnan, corresponded with the alarming circumstances in which they were placed.

The state of the President seems to have been very like what it had been in former times at Strasburg and at Boulogne, and what it was years afterwards at Magenta and Solferino.* He did not on any of these five occasions so give way to fear as to prove that he had less self-control in moments of danger than the common run of peaceful citizens; but on all of them he showed that, though he had chosen to set himself heroic tasks, his temperament was ill-fitted for the hour of battle and for the crisis of an adventure. For, besides that (in common with the bulk of mankind) he was without resource and presence of mind when he imagined that danger was really quite close upon him, his complexion and the dismal looks he wore in times of trial were always against him. From some defect perhaps in the structure of the heart or the artorial system, his skin, when he was in a state of alarm, was liable to be suffused with a greenish hue. This discoloration might be a sign of high moral courage, because it would tend to show that the spirit was warring with the flesh; but still it does not indicate that condition of body and soul which belongs to a true king of men in the hour of danger, and enables him to give heart and impulsion to those around him. It is obvious, too, that an appearance of this sort would be damping to the ardour of the bystanders. Several incidents show that between the 2d and the 4th of December the President was ir-

---

* See Note in the Appendix.

CHAP. XIV.

resolute, and keenly alive to his danger. The long-pondered plan of election which he had promulgated on the 2d of December he withdrew the next day, in obedience to the supposed desire of the Parisian multitude. He took care to have always close to his side the immense force of cavalry, to which he looked as the means of protecting his flight; and it seems that, during a great portion of the critical interval, the carriages and horses required for his escape were kept ready for instant use in the stable-yard of the Elysée. Moreover, it was at this time that he suffered himself to resort to the almost desperate resource of counterfeiting the names of men represented as belonging to the Consultative Commission. But perhaps his condition of mind may be best inferred from the posture in which history catches him whilst he nestled under the wing of the army.

He gave all he had to the soldiers.

When a peaceful citizen is in grievous peril, and depending for his life upon the whim of soldiers, his instinct is to take all his gold and go and offer it to the armed men, and tell them he loves and admires them. What, in such stress, the endangered citizen would be impelled by his nature to do, is exactly what Louis Bonaparte did. The transaction could not be concealed, and the imperial historian seems to have thought that, upon the whole, the best course was to give it an air of classic grandeur by describing the soldiers as the "conquerors" of a rugged Greek word, and by calling a French coin an "obolus." "There remained," said he, "to the

"President, out of all his personal fortune, out of all "his patrimony, a sum of fifty thousand francs. He "knew that in certain memorable circumstances the "troops had faltered in the presence of insurrection, "more from being famished than from being de-"feated; so he took all that remained to him, even "to his last crown-piece, and charged Colonel Fleury "to go to the soldiers, conquerors of demagogy, and "distribute to them, brigade by brigade, and man by "man, this his last obolus."* The President had said, in one of his addresses to the army of Paris, that he would not bid them advance, but would himself go the foremost and ask them to follow him. If it was becoming to address empty playactor's words of that sort to real soldiers, it certainly was not the duty of the President to act upon them; for there could not well be any such engagement in the streets of Paris as would make it right for a literary man (though he was also the chief of the State) to go and affect to put himself at the head of an army inured to war; but still there was a contrast between what was said and what was done, which makes a man smile as he passes. The President had vowed he would lead the soldiers against the foe, and instead, he sent them all his money. There is no reason to suppose that the change of plan was at all displeasing to the troops; and this bribing of the armed men is only adverted to here as a means of getting at the real state of the

* Granier de Cassaignac, vol. ii. p. 481.

46 TRANSACTIONS WHICH

CHAP. XIV.

President's mind, and thereby tracing up to its cause the massacre of the 4th of December.

He even signed the decree of the 5th of December.

Another clue, leading the same way, is to be found in the Decree by which the President enacted that combats with insurgents at home should count for the honour and profit of the troops in the same way as though they were fought against a foreign enemy.* It is true that this decree was not issued until the massacre of the 4th was over, but of course the temper in which a man encounters danger is to be gathered in part from his demeanour immediately after the worst moment of trial; and when it is found that the chief of a proud and mighty nation was capable of putting his hand to a paper of this sort on the 5th of December, some idea may be formed of what his sensations were on the noon of the day before, when the agony of being in fear had not as yet been succeeded by the indecorous excitement of escape.

State of Jerome Bonaparte.

Whilst Prince Louis Bonaparte was hugging the knees of the soldiers, his uncle Jerome Bonaparte fell into so painful a condition as to be unable to maintain his self-control, and he suffered himself to publish a letter in which he not only disclosed his alarm, but even showed that he was preparing to separate himself from his nephew; for he made it appear (as he could do, perhaps, with strict truth) that although he had got into danger by showing

---

* Decree of the 5th, inserted in the "Moniteur" of the 7th Dec.

himself in public with the President on the 2d of December, he was innocent of the plot, and a stranger to the counsels of the Elysée.* His son (now called Prince Napoleon) was really, they say, a strong disapprover of the President's acts, and it was natural that he should be most unwilling to be put to death or otherwise ill-treated upon the theory that he was the cousin and therefore the accomplice of Louis, for of that theory he wholly and utterly denied the truth. Any man, however firm, might well resolve that, happen what might to him, he would struggle hard to avoid being executed by mistake; and it seems unfair to cast blame on Prince Napoleon for trying to disconnect his personal destiny from that of the endangered men at the Elysée, whose counsels he had not shared. Still, the sense of being cast loose by the other Bonapartes could not but be discouraging to Prince Louis, and to those who had thrown in their lot with him.

<small>CHAP. XIV.</small>

<small>Natural anxiety of Napoleon, son of Jerome.</small>

Maupas, or De Maupas, was a man of a fine, large, robust frame, and with florid, healthy looks; but it sometimes happens that a spacious and strong-

<small>Bodily state of Maupas.</small>

---

* The letter will be found in the "Annual Register." It seems to have been sent at 10 o'clock at night on the 4th of December; but the writer evidently did not know that the insurrection at that time was so near its end as it really was, and his letter may therefore be taken as a fair indication of the state of his mind in the earlier part of the day. The advice and the mild remonstrance contained in the letter might have been given in private by a man who had not lost his calm, but the fact of allowing such a letter to be public discloses Jerome's motives.

CHAP. XIV.

looking body of that sort is not so safe a tabernacle as it seems for man's troubled spirit. It is said that the bodily strength of Maupas collapsed in the hour of danger, and that, at a critical part of the time between the night of the 2d of December and the massacre of the 4th, he had the misfortune to fall ill.

Finally, it must be repeated that on that 4th of December the army of Paris was kept in a state of inaction during all the precious hours which elapsed between the earliest dawn of the morning and two o'clock in the afternoon.

Grounds for the anxiety of the plotters, and of Magnan and the generals under him.

These are signs that the brethren of the Elysée were aghast at what they had done, and aghast at what they had to do. And it is obvious that Magnan and the twenty Generals who had embraced one another on the 27th of November, were now more involved in the danger of the plot than at first they might have expected to be; for the isolation in which the President was left, for want of men of character and station who would consent to come and stand round him, must have made all these Generals feel that even the sovereign warrant of "an order from "the Minister of War" was a covering which had become very thin.

Effect of anxious suspense upon French troops.

Now by nature the French people are used to go in flocks; and in their army there is not that social difference between the officers and the common soldiers which is the best contrivance hitherto discovered for intercepting the spread of a panic or any other bewildering impulse. With their troops, any impulse, whether of daring or fear, will often dart like lightning from man to man, and quickly involve the whole mass. Generally, perhaps, a panic in an army ascends from the ranks. On this day, the panic, it seems, went downwards. For six hours the army had been kept waiting and waiting under arms within a few hundred yards of the barricades which it was to attack. The order to advance did not come. Somewhere there was hesitation, and the Generals could not but know that even a little hesitation at such a time was both a sign and a cause of danger; but when they saw it continuing through all the morning hours of a short December day, they could hardly have failed to apprehend that the plot of the Elysée was collapsing for want of support, and they could not but know that, if this dread were well founded, their fate was likely to be a hard one.

The temperament of Frenchmen is better fitted for the hour of combat than for the endurance of this sort of protracted tension; and the anxiety of men of their race, when they are much perturbed and kept in long suspense, will easily degenerate into that kind of alarm which is apt to become ferocious. This was the kind of stress to which the troops were put on that 4th of December; and in the case of Magnan and the Generals under him, the pangs of having to wait upon the brink of action for more than two-thirds of a day were sharpened by a sense of political danger;

CHAP. XIV.

for they felt that if, after all, the scheme of the Elysée should fail, their meeting of the 27th might cause them to be brought to trial. Any one knowing what those twenty-one Generals had on their minds, and being also somewhat used to the French army, will almost be able to hear the grinding of the teeth and the rumbling of the curses which mark the armed Frenchman, when he rages because he is anxious. Even without the utterance of any words, the countenances of men thus disturbed would be swiftly read in a body of French troops; and though the soldiery and the inferior officers would not be able to make out very well what it was that was troubling the minds of the Generals, the sense of not knowing all would only make them the more susceptible of infection. On the other hand, it is certain that the instructions given to the troops prescribed the ruthless slaughtering of all who resisted or obstructed them; and although it is of course true that these directions would not compel or sanction the slaughter of peaceful crowds not at all obstructing the troops, still they would so act upon the minds of the soldiery that any passion which might chance to seize them would be likely to take a fierce shape.

Surmised cause of the massacre.

Upon the whole, then, it would seem that the natural and well-grounded alarm which beset the President and some of his associates was turned to anxiety of the raging sort when it came upon the military commanders, and that from them it ran down, till at last it seized upon the troops with so maddening a power as to cause them to face round without word of command, and open fire upon a crowd of gazing men and women.

If this solution were accepted, it would destroy the theory which ascribes to Prince Louis Bonaparte the malign design of contriving a slaughter on the Boulevard as a means of striking terror, and so crushing resistance; but it would still remain true that although it was not specifically designed and ordered, the massacre was brought about by him, and by Morny, Maupas, and St Arnaud, — all acting with the concurrence and under the encouragement of Fleury and Persigny. By them the deeds of the 2d of December were contrived and done; by them, and in order to the support of those same deeds, the army was brought into the streets; by their industry the minds of the soldiery were whetted for the slaughter of the Parisians; and, finally, by their hesitation, or the hesitation of Magnan their instrument, the army, when it was almost face to face with the barricades, was still kept standing and expectant, until its Generals, catching and transmitting in an altered form the terror which had come upon them from the Elysée, brought the troops into that state of truculent panic which was the immediate cause of the slaughter. It must also be remembered that the doubt which I have tried to solve extends only to the cause which brought about the massacre of the

CHAP. XIV.

peaceful crowds on the Boulevard; for it remains unquestioned that the killing of the prisoners taken in the barricaded quarter was the result of design, and was enforced by stringent orders. Moreover, the persons who had the blood upon their hands were the persons who got the booty. St Arnaud is no more; but Louis Napoleon Bonaparte, Morny, Fleury, Maupas, Magnan, and Persigny — all these are yet alive, and in their possession the public treasures of France may still be abundantly found.

It is known that the most practised gamesters grow weary sometimes of their long efforts to pry into the future which chance is preparing for them, and that in the midst of their anxiety and doubt they are now and then glad to accept guidance from the blind, confident guess of some one who is younger and less jaded than themselves; and when a hot-headed lad insists that he can govern fortune, when he "calls the main," as though it were a word of command, and shakes the dice-box with a lusty arm, the pale doubting elders will sometimes follow the lead of youth's high animal spirits; and if they do this and win, their hearts are warm to the lad whose fire and wilfulness compelled them to run the venture.

Gratitude due to Fleury.

Whether it be true, as is said, that in the hour of trial any of the brethren of the Elysée were urged forward by Colonel Fleury's threats, or whether, abstaining from actual violence, he was able to drive them on by the sheer ascendancy of a more ardent and resolute nature, it is certain that he well earned their gratitude, if by any means, gentle or rough, he forced them to keep their stake on the table. For they won — they won France. They used her hard; they took her freedom; they laid open her purse, and were rich with her wealth. They went and sat in the seats of Kings and Statesmen, and handled the mighty nation as they willed in the face of Europe. Those who hated freedom, and those also who bore ill-will towards the French people, made merry with what they saw. {CHAP. XIV. *The use the Elysée made of France.*}

These are the things which Charles Louis Napoleon Bonaparte did. What he had sworn to do was set forth in the oath which he took on the 20th of December 1848. On that day he stood before the National Assembly, and, lifting his right arm towards heaven, thus swore: — "In the presence of "God, and before the French people represented by "the National Assembly, I swear to remain faithful "to the democratic Republic one and indivisible, and "to fulfil all the duties which the Constitution im-"poses upon me." What he had pledged his honour to do was set forth in the promise, which of his own free will he addressed to the Assembly. Reading from a paper which he had prepared, he uttered these words: — "The votes of the nation, and the "oath which I have just taken, command my future "conduct. My duty is clear; I will fulfil it as a "man of honour. I shall regard as enemies of the {*The oath which the President had taken.* *His added promise as a "man of honour."*}

CHAP. XIV.

The Te Deum.

"country all those who endeavour to change by illegal means that which all France has established."

In Europe at that time there were many men, and several millions of women, who truly believed that the landmarks which divided good from evil were in charge of priests, and that what Religion blessed must needs be right. Now on the thirtieth day computed from the night of the 2d of December, the rays of twelve thousand lamps pierced the thick wintry fog that clogged the morning air, and shed their difficult light through the nave of the historic pile which stands marking the lapse of ages and the strange checkered destiny of France. There waiting, there were the bishops, priests, and deacons of the Roman branch of the Church of Jesus Christ. These bishops, priests, and deacons stood thus expecting, because they claimed to be able to conduct the relations between man and his Creator; and the swearer of the oath of the 20th of December had deigned to apprise them that again, with their good leave, he was coming into "the presence of God." And he came. Where the kings of France had knelt, there was now the persistent manager of the company that had played at Strasburg and Boulogne, and with him, it may well be believed, there were Morny rejoicing in his gains, and Magnan soaring high above sums of four thousand pounds, and Maupas no longer in danger, and St Arnaud formerly Le Roy, and Fialin, more often called "Persigny," and

Fleury the propeller of all, more eager, perhaps, to go and be swift to spend his winnings, than to sit in a cathedral and think how the fire of his temperament had given him a strange power over the fate of a nation. When the Church perceived that the swearer of the oath and all his associates were ready, she began her service. Having robes whereon all down the back there was embroidered the figure of a cross, and being, it would seem, without fear, the bishops and priests went up to the high altar, and scattered rich incense, and knelt and rose, and knelt and rose again. Then, in the hearing of thousands, there pealed through the aisles that hymn of praise which purports to waft into heaven the thanksgivings of a whole people for some new and signal mercy vouchsafed to them by Almighty God. It was because of what had been done to France within the last thirty days that the Hosannas arose in Notre Dame. Moreover, the priests lifted their voices and cried aloud, chanting and saying to the Most High, "Domine, salvum fac "Ludovicum Napoleonem" — O Lord! save Louis Napoleon.

What is good, and what is evil? and who is he that deserves the prayers of a nation? If any man, being scrupulous and devout, was moved by the events of December to ask these questions of his Church, he was answered that day in the Cathedral of our Lady of Paris.

In the next December the form of the state

CHAP. XIV.

The President becomes Emperor of the French.

system was accommodated to the reality, and the President of the Republic became what men call a "French Emperor." The style that Prince Louis thought fit to take was this: — "Napoleon the Third, "by the Grace of God, and by the will of the people, "Emperor of the French."

The inaction of great numbers of Frenchmen at the time when their country was falling.

Of course, when any one thinks of the events of December 1851, the stress of his attention is apt to be brought to bear upon those who were actors, and upon those who, desiring to act, were only hindered from doing so by falling into the pits which the trappers had dug for them; but no one will fail to see that one of the main phenomena of the time was the wilful acquiescence of great numbers of men. It may seem strange that during a time of danger the sin of inaction should be found in a once free and always brave people. The cause of this was the hatred which men had of democracy. A sheer democracy, it would seem, is so unfriendly to personal

Its cause.

liberty, and therefore so vexing or alarming, not only to its avowed political enemies, but to those also who in general are accustomed to stand aloof from public affairs, that it must needs close its frail existence as soon as there comes home a General renowned in arms who chooses to make himself King. This was always laid down as a guiding principle by those who professed to be able to draw lessons from history; but even they used to think that, until some sort of hero could be found, democratic institutions might last. France showed mankind that the mere want of such a hero as will answer the purpose is a want which can be compensated by a little ingenuity. She taught the world that when a mighty nation is under a democracy, and is threatened with doctrines which challenge the ownership and enjoyment of property, any knot of men who can get trusted with a momentary hold of the engine of State (and somebody must be so trusted), may take one of their number who never made a campaign except with counterfeit soldiers, and never fired a shot except when he fired by mistake, and may make him a dictator, a lawgiver, and an absolute monarch, with the acquiescence, if not with the approval, of a vast proportion of the people. Moreover, France proved that the transition is not of necessity a slow one; and that, when the perils of a high centralisation and a great standing army are added to the perils of a sheer democracy, then freedom, although it be hedged round and guarded by all the contrivances which clever, thoughtful, and honest Republicans can devise, may be stolen and made away with in one dark winter night, as though it were a purse or a trinket.

CHAP. XIV.

Although France lost her freedom, it would be an error to imagine that upon the ruins of the commonwealth there was founded a monarchy like that, for instance, which governs the people of Russia. In empires of that kind the Sovereign commands the services of all his subjects. In France, for the most

The gentlemen of France resolved to stand aloof from the Government.

part, the gentlemen of the country resolved to stand aloof from the Government, and not only declined to vouchsafe their society to the new occupant of the Tuileries, but even looked cold upon any stray person of their own station who suffered himself to be tempted thither by money. They were determined to abide their time, and in the meanwhile to do nothing which would make it inconsistent for them, as soon as it suited their policy, to take an opportunity of laying cruel hands on the new Emperor and his associates. It was obvious that, because of the instinct which makes creatures cling to life, a monarch thus kept always standing on the very edge of a horrible fate, but still having for the time in his hands the engine of the State, would be driven by the very law of his being to make use of the forces of the nation as means of safety for himself and his comrades; and that to that one end, not only the operations of the Home Government, but even the foreign policy of the country, would be steadily aimed. And so it happened. After the 2d December in the year 1851, the foreign policy of France was used for a prop to prop the throne which Morny and his friends had built up.

Therefore, although I have dwelt awhile upon a singular passage in the domestic history of France, I have not digressed. The origin of the war with Russia could not be traced without showing what was the foreign policy of France at the time when the mischief was done; and since it happened that the foreign policy of France was new to the world, and was governed in all things by the personal exigencies of those who wielded it, no one could receive a true impression of its aim and purpose without first gathering some idea of the events by which the destinies of Europe were connected with the hopes and fears of Prince Louis and Morny and Fleury, of Magnan and Persigny and Maupas and Monsieur Le Roy St Arnaud.

CHAPTER XV.

Immediate effect of the coup d'état upon the tranquillity of Europe.

ALMOST instantly the change which was wrought by these French transactions began to act upon Europe. The associates of the Elysée well understood that if they had been able to trample upon France and her laws, their success had been made possible by the dread which the French people had of a return to tumult; and it was clear that, until they could do something more than merely head the police of the country, their new power would be hardly more stable than the passing terrors on which it rested. What they had to do was to distract France from thinking of her shame at home by sending her attention abroad. For their very lives' sake they had to make haste, and to pile up events which might stand between them and the past, and shelter them from the peril to which they were brought

The policy which it necessitated.

whenever men's thoughts were turned to the night of the 2d of December, and the Thursday, the day of blood. There could be no hesitating about this. Ambition had nothing to do with it. It was matter of life and death. If Prince Louis and Morny and Fleury, if Maupas, St Arnaud, and Magnan, were to continue quartered upon France instead of being thrown into prison and brought to trial, it was indispensable that Europe should be disturbed. Without delay the needful steps were taken.

It must have been within a week or two after the completion of the arrangements consequent on the night of the 2d of December, that the despatches went from Paris which caused M. de Lavalette to wring from the Porte the Note of the 9th of February,* and forced the Sultan into engagements unfair and offensive to Russia. The French President steadily continued this plan of driving the Porte into a quarrel with the Czar, until at length he succeeded in bringing about the event** which was followed by the advance of the Russian armies; but the moment the Czar was wrought up into a state of anger which sufficed to make him a disturber of Europe, Prince Louis, now Emperor of the French, sagaciously perceived that it might be possible for him to take violent means of appeasing the very troubles which he himself had just raised; and to do this by suddenly declaring for a conservative policy in Turkey and offering to put himself in concert with one of the great settled States of Europe. England, he knew, had always clung to a conservative policy in the East. France, he also knew, of late years, had generally done the reverse, but then France was ut-

The French Government coerced the Sultan into measures offensive to Russia.

And then sought an alliance with England.

---

* 1852. See *ante*.
** The delivery of the key and the star to the Latin monks at Bethlehem in December 1852. See *ante*.

CHAP. XV.

terly in his power; and it seemed to him that, by offering to thrust France into an English policy, he might purchase for himself an alliance with the Queen, and win for his new throne a sanction of more lasting worth than Morny's well-warranted return of his eight millions of approving Frenchmen. Above all, if he could be united with England he might be able to enter upon that conspicuous action in Europe which was needful for his safety at home, and might do this without bringing upon himself any war of a dangerous kind.

Personal feelings of the new Emperor.

Another motive of a narrower sort was urging him in the same direction. Hating freedom, hating the French people, and delighting in an incident which he looked upon as reducing the theory of Representative Government to the absurdum, Nicholas had approved and enjoyed the treatment inflicted upon France by throwing her into the felon's van and sending her to jail; but he had objected to the notion of the second Napoleon being called "the "Third;"* and, in a spirit still more pedantic, he

---

* It is said, I know not with what truth, that the style of the new Emperor was the result of a clerical error. In the course of its preparations for constituting the Empire, the Home Office wished the country to take up a word which should be intermediate between "President" and "Emperor;" so the minister determined to order that France should suddenly burst into a cry of "Vive Napoleon!" and he wrote, they say, the following order, "Que le mot d'ordre soit Vive Napoleon!!!" The clerk, they say, mistook the three notes of admiration for Roman numerals; and in a few hours the forty thousand communes of France had cried out so obediently for "Napoleon III.," that the Government was obliged to adopt the clerk's blunder.

had refused to address the French sovereign in the accustomed form. He would call him his "good "friend," but no earthly power should make him add the word "brother." The taunting society of Petersburg amused itself with the amputated phrase, and loved to call the ruler of France their "good "friend." The new Emperor chafed at this, for his vanity was hurt; but he abided his time.

At length, nay so early as the 28th of January 1853, the French Emperor perceived that his measures had effectually roused the Czar's hostility to the Sultan, and he instantly proposed to England that the two Powers should act together in extinguishing the flames which he himself had just kindled, and should endeavour to come to a joint understanding, with a view to resist the ambition of Russia. Knowing beforehand what the policy of England was, he all at once adopted it, and proposed it to our Government in the very terms always used by English statesmen. He took, as it were, an "old copy" of the first English speech from the throne which came to his hand, and, following its words, declared that the first object should be to "preserve the integrity of the Ottoman Empire."* From that moment until the summer of 1855, and perhaps even down to a still later period, he did not once swerve from the great scheme of forming and maintaining an offensive alliance with England

The French Emperor's scheme for superseding the concord of the four Powers by drawing England into a separate alliance with himself.

---

* "Eastern Papers," part I. p. 69.

against the Czar, and to that object he subordinated all other considerations. He had at that time the rare gift of being able to keep himself alive to the proportionate value of political objects. He knew how to give up the less for the sake of attaining and keeping the greater. Governed by this principle, he gradually began to draw closer and closer towards England; and when the angry Czar imagined that he was advancing in the cause of his Church against a resolute champion of the Latins, his wily adversary was smiling perhaps with Lord Cowley about the "key" and the "cupola," and preparing to form an alliance on strictly temporal grounds.

It would have been well for Europe if the exigences of the persons then wielding the destinies of France would have permitted the State to rest content with that honest share of duty which fell to the lot of each of the four Powers when the intended occupation of the Principalities was announced. Neither the interest nor the honour of France required that in the Eastern Question she should stand more forward than any other of the remonstrant States; but the personal interest of the new Emperor and his December friends did not at all coincide with the interest of France; for what he and his associates wanted, and what in truth they really needed, was to thrust France into a conflict which might be either diplomatic or warlike, but which was at all events to be of a conspicuous sort, tending to ward off the peril of home politics, and give to the fabric of the 2d of December something like station and celebrity in Europe. In order to achieve this, it clearly would not suffice for France to be merely one of a conference of four great Powers quietly and temperately engaged in repressing the encroachment of the Czar. Her part in such a business could not possibly be so prominent nor so animating as to draw away the attention of the French from the persons who had got into their palaces and their offices of State. On the other hand, a close, separate, and significant alliance with England, and with England alone, to the exclusion of the rest of the four Powers, would not only bring about the conflict which was needed for the safety and comfort of the Tuileries, but would seem in the eyes of the mistaken world to give the sanction of the Queen's pure name to the acts of the December night and the Thursday the day of blood. The unspeakable value of this moral shelter to persons in the condition of the new French Monarch, and St Arnaud, Morny, and Maupas, can never be understood except by those who look back and remember how exalted the moral station of England was, in the period which elapsed between the 10th of April 1848 and the time when she suffered herself to become entangled in engagements with the French Emperor.

It would have been right enough that France and England, as the two great maritime Powers, should have come to an understanding with each other in regard to the disposition of their fleets; but even if they had been concerting for only that limited purpose, it would have been right that the general tenor and object of their naval arrangements should have received the antecedent approval of the two other Powers with whom they were in cordial agreement. The English Government, however, not only consented to engage in naval movements which affected — nay, actually governed — the question of peace or war, but fell into the error of concerting these movements with France alone, and doing this not because of any difference which had arisen between the four Powers, but simply because France and England were provided with ships; so that in truth the Western Powers, merely because they were possessed of the implement which enabled them to put a pressure upon the Czar, resolved to act as though they were the only judges of the question whether the pressure should be applied or not; and this at a time when, as Lord Clarendon declared in Parliament, the four Powers were "all acting cor-"dially together." Of course, this wanton segregation tended to supersede or dissolve the concord which bound the four Powers, and, as a sure consequence, to endanger yet more than ever the cause of peace. Some strange blindness prevented Lord Aberdeen from seeing the path he trod, or rather prevented him from seeing it with a clearness conducive to action. But what the French Emperor wanted was even more than this, and what he wanted was done. It is true that neither admiration nor moral disapproval of the conduct of princes ought to have any exceeding sway over our relations with foreign States; and if we had had the misfortune to find that the Emperor of the French was the only potentate in Europe whose policy was in accord with our own, it might have been right that closer relations of alliance with France (however humiliating they might seem in the eyes of the moralist) should have followed our separation from the other States of Europe. But no such separation had occurred. What the French Emperor ventured to attempt, and what he actually succeeded in achieving, was to draw England into a distinct and separate alliance with himself, not at a time when she was isolated, but at a moment when she was in close accord with the rest of the four Powers.

Towards the close of the Parliamentary session of 1853, the determination on the part of Austria to rid the Principalities of their Russian invaders was growing in intensity. Prussia also was firm; and in principle the concord of the four Powers was so exact, that it extended, as was afterwards seen, not only to the terms on which the difference between Russia and Turkey should be settled, but to the ulterior arrangements which might be pressed upon Russia at the conclusion of the war which she was provoking. "The four great Powers," said Lord Aberdeen on the 12th of August, "are now acting

CHAP. XV.

The nature of the understanding of Midsummer 1853 between France and England.

"in concert."* "In all these transactions," said Lord Clarendon,** "Austria, England, Prussia, and "France are all acting cordially together, in order "to check designs which they consider inconsistent "with the balance of power, and with those terri-"torial limits which have been established by various "treaties."

Yet it cannot be doubted that in the midst of this perfect concord of the four Powers, the English Government was induced to enter into a separate understanding with the Emperor of the French.*** This was the fatal transaction which substituted a cruel war for the peaceful but irresistible pressure which was exerted by the four Powers. The purport of this arrangement still lurks in private notes, and in recollections of private interviews; but it can be seen that (for reasons never yet explained) France and England were engaging to move in advance of the other Powers. The four Powers, being all of one mind, were still to remain in concert so far as concerned the discussion and adjudication of the questions pending between Russia and Turkey; but France and England were to volunteer to enforce their judgment. The four Powers were to be judges, and two of them — namely, France and England — were to be the executioners. What made this arrangement the more preposterous, was that the

---

* 129 Hansard, p. 1650.
** Ibid. p. 1423.
*** Ibid. pp. 1424, 1768, 1826.

outrage of which Europe complained was the occupation of two provinces which abutted upon the Austrian dominions. Of all the great Powers, Austria was the chief sufferer. Austria was upon the spot. Austria was the one Power which instantly and in a summary way could force the Czar to quit his hold; and yet the charge of undertaking a duty which pressed upon her more than upon any other State in Europe, was voluntarily taken upon themselves by two States whose dominions were vastly distant from the scene of the evil deed. It was much as though the forces of the United States and of Brazil were to come across the Atlantic to defend Antwerp from the French, whilst the English looked on and thanked their enterprising friends for relieving them of their duty.

There was not, perhaps, more than one of the members of the English Cabinet who desired the formation of this singular alliance on grounds like those which moved the French Emperor; and it is believed that Lord Aberdeen and several other members of the Government were much governed by a shallow theory which had prevailed for some years amongst public men. The theory was, that close union between France and England was a security for the peace of Europe. "Sure I am," said one confident man, who echoed the crude thought of many—"sure I am, that if the advisers of the Crown "in this country act in cordial concert with the "Government of the Emperor of the French, and if "the forces of the two countries in the Mediterranean "are to act in concert, then it will be almost im"possible that any war can disturb the peace of "Europe." But of course, to men of more statesmanlike views, the main temptation was the prospect of seeing France dragged into the policy which England had always entertained upon the Eastern Question.

Perhaps it will be thought that the practice of hiding away momentous engagements between States in the folds of private notes may now and then justify an endeavour to infer the nature of an agreement secretly made between two Governments from the tenor of their subsequent actions, and from a knowledge of surrounding facts. If this licence were to be granted, and if also it were to be assumed that the English as well as the French Government was negotiating with open eyes, it might perhaps be laid down that the compact of Midsummer 1853 was virtually of this sort: — "The Emperor of the "French shall set aside the old views of the French "Foreign Office, and shall oblige France with all "her forces to uphold the Eastern policy of England. "In consideration of this sacrifice of French interests "by the French Emperor, England promises to give "her moral sanction (in the way hereinafter pre"scribed) to the arrangements of December 1851, and "to take the following means for strengthening the "throne and endeavouring to establish the dynasty "of the Emperor of the French: 1st, England shall

"give up the system of peaceful coercion which is
"involved in the concerted action of the four Powers,
"and shall adopt, in lieu of it, a separate under-
"standing with France, of such a kind as to place
"the two Powers conspicuously in advance of the
"others, and in a state of more immediate antagonism
"to Russia with a prospect of eventual war. 2d, Even
"before any treaty of alliance is agreed upon, the
"Queen of England shall declare before all Europe
"that the Emperor of the French is united with Her
"Majesty in her endeavours to allay the troubles
"now threatening Europe with war; and it shall not
"be competent to the English Government to weaken
"the effect of this announcement by advising Her
"Majesty to include any other Sovereigns in the
"same statement. If Her Majesty should continue
"to be closely in accord with the rest of the four
"Powers, she may be advised to speak of them in
"general terms as her allies, but they are not to be
"named. 3d, If hostilities should become necessary,
"the two Governments will determine upon the
"measures to be adopted in common; and in that
"case also it is distinctly understood that the English
"Government will advise the Queen not to shrink
"from the gratification of receiving the Emperor of
"the French as her guest. It is, of course, to be
"understood (*il va sans dire*) that the reception of
"His Majesty at the English Court is to be in all
"respects the same as would be the reception of any
"other great Sovereign in alliance with the Queen.

CHAP.
XV.

"Whenever occasion requires it, the other actors in "the operations of December 1851 shall be received "and treated by the English authorities with the "honours due to the trusted servants of a friendly "Power, and without objections founded on the trans-"actions of December, or any of the circumstances "of their past lives." These are only imaginary words, but they show what the French Emperor was seeking to achieve, and they represent but too faithfully what the English Government did.

Every State is entitled to regard a foreign nation as represented by its Government. The principle is a sound one; but it must be owned that by this alliance the theory was pushed to an ugly conclusion. What happened was the like of this:—There came to us five men heavily laden with treasure, but looking hurried and anxious. They wanted to speak to us. Upon inquiring who they were, and comparing their answers with our other means of knowing the truth, we found that two of them bore names resulting in the usual way from marriages and baptisms,* and that the other three had been going by names which they had chosen for the sake of euphony. They said that suddenly they had become so struck with the soundness of our old-fashioned opinions, that they asked nothing better than to be suffered to devote the immense resources which they could command to the attainment of the object which

* These two were Prince Louis Bonaparte and Maupas.

we had always desired. All they wanted, in return, was that, in pursuing our own object side by side with them, we would promise not to suffer ourselves to be clogged by our old scruples against breaches of the peace; that we would admit them to our intimacy, allowing ourselves to be much seen with them in public; and that, in order to make our favour the more signal, we would consent to turn aside a little from our old friends: that was all. With regard to the question of how they had come by their treasure, and all the vast resources they offered us, their story was that they had all these things with the express consent of the former owner. There was something about them which made us fear that, if we repulsed them, they would carry their treasures to the very man who, at that moment, was giving us trouble. In truth, it seemed that, either from us or from somebody else, they must and they would have shelter. Upon their hands there was a good deal of blood. We shrank a little, but we were tempted much. We yielded: we struck the bargain. What we did was not unlawful, for those with whom we treated had for the time a real hold upon the people in whose great name they professed to come; and by the custom of nations we were entitled to say that we would know nothing of any France except the France that was brought to us by these five persons to be disposed of for the purposes of our "Eastern Question;" but when we had done this

CHAP. XV.

Announcement of it to Parliament.

Failure of Parliament to understand the real import of the disclosure.

The Queen's Speech, August 1853.

thing, we had no right to believe that to Europe at large, still less to the gentlemen of France, the fair name of England would seem as it seemed before.

But whatever were the terms of the understanding between the two Governments, the result of it was that the English Cabinet, disregarding the policy which only six days before had united it in a concerted action with the Powers represented at the Conference, now announced, through the lips of Lord Palmerston,* "that England and France were "agreed, that they continued to follow the same "policy, and that they had the most perfect confidence "in each other." These words were enough to show any one used to foreign affairs that England was advancing with France into an adventurous policy, and then (though even then they were dangerously late) Members of Parliament might have stood forward with some hope of being able to check their country in her smooth descent from peace to war. They lost the occasion; it did not recur.

At the close of the session, the Queen's Speech announced to Europe "that the Emperor of the "French had united with Her Majesty in earnest "endeavours to reconcile differences, the continuance "of which might involve Europe in war; and she "declared that, acting in concert with her Allies, and "relying on the exertions of the Conference then

* 8th July 1853, in the House of Commons.

"assembled at Vienna, Her Majesty had good reason to hope that an honourable arrangement would speedily be accomplished."*

It would seem, at first sight, that this language had been occasioned by some accidental displacement of words; and that it could not have been intended for the Queen of England to say that she was acting in concert with her Allies assembled at Vienna, and to declare, in another limb of the same sentence, that she was "united" with one of them. Unhappily, the error was not an error of words. The Speech accurately described the strange policy which our Government had adopted; for it was strictly true that, in the midst of a perfect concord between the four great Powers, the English Cabinet had been drawn into a separate union with France, and into an union of such a kind as to require the distinguishing phrase which disclosed the new league to Europe.

This Speech from the Throne may be regarded as marking the point where the roads of policy branched off. By the one road, England, moving in company with the rest of the four Powers, might insure a peaceful repression of the outrage which was disturbing Europe; by the other, she might also enforce the right, but, joined with the French Emperor, and parted from the rest of the four Powers, she would

This marks where the roads to peace and to war branched off.

* 129 Hansard, p. 1826.

CHAP. XV. reach it by passing through war. The Cabinet of Lord Aberdeen desired peace, and not war; but, seeing dimly, they took the adventurous path. They so little knew whither they were going that they made no preparation for war.*

* See Lord Aberdeen's evidence before the Sebastopol Committee.

CHAPTER XVI.

THE difference between a servant and a Minister of State lies in this: — that the servant obeys the orders given him, without troubling himself concerning the question whether his master is right or wrong; whilst a Minister of State declines to be the instrument for giving effect to measures which he deems to be hurtful to his country. The Chancellor of the Russian Empire was sagacious and politic: and his experience in the business of the State, and in the councils of Europe, went back to the great days when Nesselrode and Hardenberg, and Metternich and Wellington set their seals to the same charter. That the Czar was wrong in these transactions against Turkey no man in Europe knew better than Count Nesselrode; and at first he had the courage to speak to his master so frankly that Nicholas, when he had heard a remark which tended to wisdom and moderation, would cry out, "That is "what the Chancellor is perpetually telling me!" But, unhappily for the Czar and for his empire, the Minister did not enjoy so commanding a station as to be able to put restraint upon his Sovereign, nor

CHAP. XVI.
Count Nesselrode.

CHAP. XVI.

even perhaps to offer him counsel in his angry mood. He could advise with Nicholas the Czar; but there were reasons which made his counsels unwelcome to a heated defender of the Greek faith. He was a member of the Church of England, and the maddening rumours of the day made out that into the jaws of this very Church of England Lord Stratford was dragging the Sultan and all his Moslem subjects. Then, too, Count Nesselrode was worldly; but, after all, the quality most certain to make him irksome to a Prince in a high state of religious or ecclesiastic excitement was his good sense. It was dangerous for a wise, able sinner like him to go near holy Nicholas the Pontiff, the Head of God's Orthodox Church upon earth, when he was hearing the voices from Heaven, when he was raging against the enemies of the Faith, and struggling to enforce his will upon mankind by utterances of the hated name of Canning,* and interjections, and gnashing of teeth. Far from being able to make a stand against this consuming fury, Nesselrode did not even decline to be the instrument for disclosing to all the world his master's condition of mind.

State of the Czar after knowing that the fleets of France and Eng-

When the Czar knew that the fleets of the Western Powers were coming up into the Levant, and that the sword of England was now in the hands of Lord Stratford, he was thrown into so fierce a state, that his notions of what was true and

---

* The Czar used to call Lord Stratford "Lord Canning."

what was not true — of what was plausible, and what was ascertainably false — of what was a cause, and what was an effect — of what happened first, and what happened last, — nay, almost, it would seem, his notions of what was the Bosphorus and what was the Hellespont,* — became as a heap of ruins. He was in the condition imagined by the Psalmist, when he prayed the Lord that his enemy might be "confounded." Count Nesselrode was forced to gather up his master's shivered thoughts, and, putting them as well as he could into the language of diplomacy, to address to all the Courts of Europe a wild remonstrance against the measures of the Western Powers. The approach of their fleets to an anchorage in the Ægean outside the Straits of the Dardanelles was treated in this despatch as though it were little less than a seizure of Constantinople; and it was represented that this was an act of violence which had entitled and compelled the Czar, in his own defence, to occupy the Principalities.** Lord Clarendon seized this weak pretence and easily laid it bare; for he showed that Nicholas, in his anger, was transposing events, and that the Czar's resolve to cross the Pruth was anterior to the occurrence which he now declared to have been the motive of his action. Then, in language worthy

---

* The despatch which gave utterance to this raving treated an anchorage in the Ægean, outside the Dardanelles, as almost a virtual occupation of Constantinople.

** "Eastern Papers," part I. p. 342.

of England, our Foreign Secretary went on to vindicate her right to send her fleets whither she chose, so long as they were on the high seas, or on the coasts of a Sovereign legitimately assenting to their presence. Nearly at the same time the writer of the French Foreign Office despatches pursued the Czar through Europe with his bright, cutting, pitiless logic.*

<small>The Vienna Conference.</small>

Of course, the vivacity of France and England tended to place Austria at her ease, and to make her more backward than she would otherwise have been in sending troops into the Banat; and, moreover, the separate action of the Western Powers was well calculated, as will be seen by-and-by, to undo the good which might be effected by the Conference of the four Powers at Vienna. The Conference, however, did not remit its labour. The mediating character which belonged to it in its original constitution was gradually changed, until at length it represented what was nothing less than a confederacy of the four Powers against Russia. It is true that it was a confederacy which sought to exhaust persuasion, and to use to the utmost the moral pressure of assembled Europe before it resorted to arms; and it is true also that it was willing to make the Czar's retreat from his false moves as easy and as free from shame as the nature of his late errors would allow: but

---

* These despatches bear the signature of M. Drouyn de Lhuys, but it was commonly believed at the time that they were written by a man on the permanent staff of the French Foreign Office.

these were views held by the English Cabinet as well as by the Conference; and it is certain that, if our Government had seen clear, and had been free from separate engagements, it would have stood fast upon the ground occupied by the four Powers, and would have refused to be drawn into measures which were destined to be continually undoing the pacific work of the diplomatists assembled at Vienna.

CHAP. XVI.

But partnership with the midnight associates of the 2d of December was a heavy yoke. With all his heart and soul Lord Aberdeen desired the tranquillity of Europe; but he had suffered his Cabinet to enter into close friendly engagements with one to whom the tranquillity of Europe portended jail, and ill-usage, and death. The French Emperor had consented to engage France in an English policy; and he thought he had a right to insist that England should pay the price, and help to give him the means of such signal action in Europe as might drive away men's thoughts from the hour when the Parliament of France had been thrown into the felons' van.

The effect upon England of becoming entangled in a separate understanding with France.

The object at which the French Emperor was aiming stands clear enough to the sight; but at this time the scheme of action by which he sought to attain his ends was ambiguous. In general, men are prone to find out consistency in the acts of rulers, and to imagine that numberless acts, appearing to have different aspects, are the result of one steady design; but those who love truth better than symmetry

The French Emperor's ambiguous scheme of action.

CHAP. XVI.

will be able to believe that much of the conduct of the French Emperor was rather the effect of clashing purposes than of duplicity. There are philosophers who imagine that the human mind (corresponding in that respect with the brain) has a dual action, and that the singleness of purpose observed in a decided man is the result of a close accord between the two engines of thought, and not of actual unity. Certainly it would appear that the Emperor Louis Napoleon, more than most other men, was accustomed to linger in doubt between two conflicting plans, and to delay his final adoption of the one, and his final rejection of the other, for as long a time as possible, in order to find out what might be best to be ultimately done by carrying on experiments for many months together with two rival schemes of action.

But whether this double method of action was the result of idiosyncrasy or of a profound policy, it was but too well fitted for the object of drawing England into a war. The aim of the French Emperor was to keep his understanding with England in full force, and yet to give the alliance a warlike direction. If he were to adopt a policy frankly warlike, he would repel Lord Aberdeen and endanger the alliance. If he were to be frankly pacific, there would be a danger of his restoring to Europe that tranquillity which could not fail to bring him and his December friends into jeopardy. In this strait he did not exactly take a middle course. By splitting his means of action he managed to take two courses at the same time.

There are people who can write at the same time with both hands. Politically, Louis Napoleon had this accomplishment. With his left hand he seemed to strive after peace; with his right he tried to stir up a war. The language of his diplomacy was pacific, and yet at the very same time he contrived that the naval forces of France and England should be used as the means of provoking a war. The part which he took in the negotiations going on at Vienna, and in the other capitals of the great Powers, was temperate, just, and moderate; and it is probable that the Despatches which indicated this spirit long continued to mislead Lord Aberdeen, and to keep him under the impression that an Anglo-French alliance was really an engine of peace; but it will be seen that, as soon as the French Emperor had drawn England into an understanding with him, he was enabled to engage her in a series of dangerous naval movements, which he contrived to keep going on simultaneously with the efforts of the negotiators, so as always to be defeating their labours.

CHAP. XVI.
His diplomacy seems pacific.
At the same time he engages England in naval movements tending to provoke war.

In order to appreciate the exceeding force of the lever which was used for this purpose, a man ought to have in his mind the political geography of south-eastern Europe, and the configuration of the seas which flow with a ceaseless current into the waters of the Ægean.

The Euxine is connected with the Mediterranean by the Straits of the Bosphorus, the Sea of Marmora, and the Straits of the Dardanelles. The Bosphorus

The Bosphorus and the Dardanelles.

CHAP. XVI.

is a current of the sea, seventeen miles in length, and in some places hardly more than half a mile broad, but so deep, even home to the shores on either side, that a ship of war can almost, as it were, find shade under the gardens of the European shore — can almost mix her spars with the cypresses which darken the coast of Asia. At its southern extremity the Bosphorus mingles with the waters of the great inlet or harbour which still often goes by the name of the Golden Horn; and at length, after passing between Constantinople and its beautiful suburb of Scutari, the Straits open out into the land-locked basin now known as the Sea of Marmora, which used to be called the Propontis. At the foot of this inland sea the water is again contracted into a deep channel, no more, in one place, than three-quarters of a mile in breadth, and is not set free till, after a course of some forty miles, it reaches the neighbourhood of the Troad, and spreads abroad into the Ægean. These last are the famous straits between Europe and Asia which used to be called the Hellespont, and are now the Dardanelles. The Bosphorus and the Dardanelles are both so narrow that, even in the early times of artillery, they could be commanded by guns on either side, and it followed that these waters had not the character of "high seas." And since the land upon either side belonged to the Ottoman Empire, the Sultans always claimed and always enjoyed a right to keep out foreign ships of war from both the straits. Now on the Black Sea

The Sultan's ancient right to control them.

Russia had as much seabord as Turkey, and nevertheless, like every other Power, she was shut out from all right to send her armed navy into the Mediterranean through the Bosphorus and the Dardanelles. There being no other outlet, her Black Sea fleet was pent up in an inland basin. Painful as this duress must needs be to a haughty State having a powerful fleet in the Euxine, it would seem that Russia has been more willing to submit to the restriction than to see the warflag of other States in the Dardanelles or the Bosphorus. The presence of a force greater than her own, or even rivalling it, did not comport with the kind of ascendancy which she was always seeking to establish at Constantinople and on the seabord of the Euxine. Russia, therefore, had been a willing party to the treaty of 1841. By this treaty the five great Powers acknowledged the right of the Sultan to exclude armed navies from both the straits; and, on the other hand, the Sultan engaged that in time of peace he would always exercise this right of exclusion. Moreover, the five Powers promised that they would all respect this engagement by the Sultan. The result, therefore, was that, whether with or without the consent of the Sultan, no foreign squadron, at a time when the Sultan was at peace, could lawfully appear in either of the straits.* But when the Emperor Nicholas forcibly occupied the Principalities. it was clear that this act

Policy of Russia in regard to the straits.

The rights of the Sultan and the five Powers under the treaty of 1841.

How these rights were affected by the Czar's seizure of the Principalities.

---

* There were exceptions in favour of vessels having on board the Representatives of foreign States.

CHAP. XVI. was a just cause of war whenever the Sultan might think fit so to treat it; and there was fair ground for saying that, even before a declaration of war, the invasion of the Sultan's dominions was such a violation of the state of peace contemplated by the treaty, that the Sultan was morally released from his engagement, and might be justified in asking his allies to send their fleets up through the straits. On the other hand, the appearance of foreign navies in the Dardanelles was regarded as so destructive to Russian ascendancy, that the bare prospect of it used to fill Russian statesmen with dismay; and the Emperor Nicholas held the idea in such horror that the mere approach of the French and English fleets to the Levant wrought him, as we have seen, to a state of mind which was only too faithfully portrayed by his Chancellor's Circular.

Powerful means of coercing the Czar.

It is plain, therefore, that the power of advising the Sultan to call up the French and English fleets was an engine of immense force in the hands of the Western Powers; but it is also certain that this was a power which would put a much harder stress upon Russia whilst it was kept suspended over her, than it was likely to do when it came to be physically used. To subject Nicholas to the fear of having to see foreign war-flags in the straits, was to apply a pressure well fitted for coercing him; but actually to exert the power was to break its spell, and to change the Czar's wholesome dread into a frenzy of anger hardly consistent with hopes of peace.

Importance of refraining from a premature use of the power.

The French Emperor had no sooner engaged the English Government in a separate understanding, than he began to insist upon the necessity of using the naval power of France and England in the way which he proposed — a way bitterly offensive to Russia. Having at length succeeded in forcing this measure upon England, he, after a while, pressed upon her another movement of the fleets still more hostile than the first, and again he succeeded in bringing the English Government to yield to him. Again, and still once again, he did the like, always in the end bringing England to adopt his hostile measures; and he never desisted from this course of action until, at last, it had effected a virtual rupture between the Czar and the Western Powers.

CHAP. XVI. The naval movements in which the French Emperor engages England.

Not yet as part of this narrative, but by way of anticipation, and in order to gather into one page the grounds of the statement just made, the following instances are given of the way in which the English Government was, from time to time, driven to join with the French Emperor in making a quarrelsome use of the two fleets: — On the 13th of July 1853, the French Emperor, through his Minister of Foreign Affairs, declared to the English Government that if the occupation of the Principalities continued, the French fleet could not longer remain at Beshika Bay. On the 19th of August he declared it to be absolutely necessary that the combined fleets should enter the Dardanelles, and he pressed the English Government to adopt a resolution to

Proofs of this drawn (in anticipation of a later part of the narrative) from transactions subsequent to the date of the Queen's Speech.

CHAP. XVI. this effect. On the 21st of September he insisted that the English Government, at the same moment as the French, should immediately order up the combined squadrons to Constantinople. On the 15th of December he pressed the English Government to agree that the Allied fleets should enter the Euxine, take possession of it, and interdict the passage of every Russian vessel. It will be seen that, with more or less reluctance and after more or less delay, these demands were always acceded to by England: and the course thus taken by the maritime Powers was fatal to the pending negotiations; for, besides that in the way already shown the Czar's wholesome fears were converted into bursts of rage, the Turks at the same time were deriving a dangerous encouragement from the sight of the French and English war-flags; and the result was, that the negotiators, with all their skill and all their patience, were never able to frame a Note in the exact words which would allay the anger of Nicholas, without encountering a steadfast resistance on the part of the Sultan.

Some men will believe that a long series of acts, all having a tendency in the same direction, and ending at length in war, were deliberately planned by the French Emperor as a means of bringing about the result which they effected, and that the temperate and sometimes conciliatory negotiations which were carried on during the same period were a mask to the real intent. It is perhaps more likely to be true that the French Emperor was all this time hesitating, and keeping his judgment in suspense. What he needed, for his very life's sake, was to become so conspicuous, whether as a disturber or as a pacificator of other nations, that Frenchmen might be brought to look at what he was doing to others instead of what he had done to them; and if he could have reached to this by seeming to take a great ascendant in the diplomacy of Europe, it is possible that, for a while at least, he might have been content to spare the world from graver troubles; but whether he acted from design or under the impulse of varying and conflicting wishes, it is certain that that command of naval power, which was an engine of excellent strength for enforcing the restoration of tranquillity, was so used, by his orders and under his persuasion, as to become the means of provoking a war.

CHAP. XVI.

Means well fitted for enforcing a just peace were so used as to provoke war.

CHAPTER XVII.

Lord Stratford's scheme of pacification.

LORD STRATFORD, it would seem, was unconscious of his power over the mind of Nicholas, and did not understand that it rested with him to determine whether the Czar should be politic or raging. He did not know that, as long as he was at Therapia, every deed, every word of the Divan was regarded as coming from the English Ambassador; and that the bare thought of the Greek Church in Turkey being under the protection of "Canning," was the very one which would at any moment change the Czar from an able man of business to an almost irresponsible being. Taking the complaints of Russia according to their avowed meaning, the English Ambassador faithfully strove to remove every trace of the foundation on which they rested; and having caused the Porte to issue firmans perpetuating all the accustomed privileges of the Greek Church, he proposed that copies of these firmans should be sent to the Court of St Petersburg, together with a courteous Note from the Porte to Count Nesselrode, distinctly assuring the Chancellor that the firmans confirmed the privileges of the

Greek Church in perpetuity, and virtually, therefore, engaging that the grants should never be revoked.* This was doing exactly what Russia ostensibly required; but it was also doing exactly that which the Czar most abhorred, for to his mind it indicated nothing less than that the Greek Church was passing under the gracious protection of Lord Stratford. The polished courtesy of the Note imparting this concession only made it the more hateful, by showing on its face whence it came. However, Lord Stratford obtained for his plan the full approval of his French, Austrian, and Prussian colleagues, as well as of the Porte; and the Note, signed by Reshid Pacha, and enclosing copies of the new firmans, was despatched to Vienna, with a view to its being thence transmitted to St Petersburg. The packet which held these papers contained the very ingredients which were best fitted for disturbing the reason of the Czar. It happened, however, that at Vienna there were men who knew something of the psychological part of the Eastern Question, and they took upon themselves to arrest the maddening Note in its transit.

And now the representatives of the four Powers, conferring in the Austrian capital, succeeded in framing a document which soon became known to Europe under the name of the "Vienna Note." This paper, framed originally in Paris, was perfected and finally

The "Vienna Note."

---

* 20th July 1853. "Eastern Papers," part II. p. 15.

CHAP. XVII.

Agreed to by the four Powers, and

Accepted by Russia.

The French Emperor does nothing to thwart the success of the Note.

approved by all the four Powers conferring at Vienna. It was a draft of a Note understood to be brought forward by Austria in her mediating capacity, and proposed to be addressed by the Porte to the Russian Government. The parties to the Conference believed that the engagements purporting to be made by the Note made on the part of the Sultan might satisfy the Czar without endangering the true interests of Turkey. Indeed, the Austrian Government, somewhat forgetting its duty as a faithful mediator, had used means of ascertaining that the Note would be acceptable to Russia,* but without taking a like step in favour of the other disputant. Copies of the Note thus framed were sent for approval to St Petersburg and to Constantinople, and the acceptance of the arrangement was pressed upon the Governments of the two disputing States with all the moral weight which the four great Powers could give to their unanimous award.

And here it ought to be marked that at this moment the French Emperor did nothing to thwart the restoration of tranquillity. He perhaps believed that if a Note which had originated in Paris were to become the basis of a settlement, he might found on this circumstance a claim to the glory of having pacified Europe, and in that wholesome way might achieve the sort of conspicuousness which he loved and needed. Perhaps he was only obeying that

* "Eastern Papers," part II. p. 27.

doubleness of mind which made him always prone to do acts clashing one with another. But whatever may have been the cause which led him for a moment to intermit his policy, it is just to acknowledge that he seems to have been faithfully willing to give effect to the means of pacification which were proffered by the "Vienna Note." It soon became known that the Note was agreed to by the Emperor Nicholas. Men believed that all was settled. It was true that the courier who was expected to be the bearer of the assent of the Porte had not yet come in from Constantinople, but it was assumed that the representatives of the four Powers had taken the precaution of possessing themselves of the real views of the Turkish Government; and, besides, it was thought impossible that the Sultan should undertake to remain in antagonism to Russia, if the support which he had hitherto received from the four great Powers were to be transferred from him to the Czar.

Those who dwell far away from great cities can hardly, perhaps, believe that the touching signs of simplicity which they observe in rural life may be easily found now and then in the councils of assembled Europe. The Governments of all the four Powers, and their representatives assembled at Vienna, fondly imagined that they could settle the dispute and restore tranquillity to Europe without consulting Lord Stratford de Redcliffe. They framed and despatched the Note without learning what his opinion of it was, and it is probable that a know-

CHAP. XVII.

Lord Stratford had not been consulted.

ledge of this singular omission may have conduced to make the Czar accept the award of the mediating Powers, by tempting him with the delight of seeing Lord Stratford overruled. But, on the other hand, the one man who was judge of what ought or ought not to be conceded by the Turks was Lord Stratford; and it is plain that any statesmen who forgot him in their reckoning must have been imperfect in their notion of political dynamics. It would be wrong to suppose that a sound judgment by the four Powers would be liable to be overturned by Lord Stratford from any mere feeling of neglect. He was too proud, as well as too honest, to be capable of such a littleness. What was to be apprehended was, that until it was ratified by the English Ambassador at the Porte, the decision of a number of men in Vienna and Paris and London and Berlin might turn out to be really erroneous, or might seem to be so in the eyes of one who was profoundly versed in the subject; and no man had a right to make sure that, even at the instance of all Europe, this strong-willed Englishman would consent to use his vast personal ascendancy as a means of forcing upon the Turks a surrender which he held to be dangerous.

Early in August the Vienna Note reached Constantinople; and the Turkish Government soon detected in it not only a misrecital of history, but words of a dangerous sort, conveying or seeming to convey to Russia, under a new form, that very pro-

tectorate of the Greek Church in Turkey which had CHAP. XVII.
brought about the rupture of the negotiation conducted by Prince Mentschikoff. The four Powers, however, had determined to press the acceptance of the arrangement upon the Porte; and on the 12th it became known at Constantinople that the Note had been accepted by the Emperor Nicholas. On the same day the English Ambassador received instructions from London, which informed him that the English Government "adhered to the Vienna "Note, and considered that it fully guarded the principle which had been contended for, and might "therefore with perfect safety be signed by the "Porte;" and Lord Clarendon went on to express a hope that the Ambassador would have "found no "difficulty in procuring the assent of the Turkish "Government to a project which the allies of the "Sultan unanimously concurred in recommending for "his adoption." *

The "Vienna "Note" in the hands of Lord Stratford.

It cannot be doubted that Lord Stratford's opinion as to the effect of the Vienna Note was opposed to that of his Government,** but it was his duty to obey. He obeyed. He "scrupulously abstained from ex-"pressing any private opinion of his on the Note "whilst it was under consideration at the Porte," and he conveyed to the Turkish Government the desire of Europe. "I called the attention of Reshid Pasha," said he, "to the strong and earnest manner in which

* "Eastern Papers," part II. p. 27.
** Ibid. pp. 72, 82.

"the Vienna Note was recommended to the acceptance
"of the Porte, not only by Her Majesty's Government,
"but also by the Cabinets of Austria, France, and
"Prussia. I reminded him of the intelligence which
"had been received from St Petersburg, purporting
"that the Emperor of Russia had signified his readiness
"to accept the same Note. I urged the importance
"of his engaging the Porte to come to a decision with
"the least possible delay. I repeatedly urged the
"importance of an immediate decision, and the danger
"of declining, or only accepting with amendments,
"what the four friendly Powers so earnestly recom-
"mended, and what the Cabinet of St Petersburg had
"accepted in its actual state."*

These were dutiful words. But it is not to be believed that, even if he strove to do so, Lord Stratford could hide his real thoughts from the Turkish Ministers. There was that in his very presence which disclosed his volition; for if the thin disciplined lips moved in obedience to constituted authorities, men who knew how to read the meaning of his brow, and the light which kindled beneath, would gather that the Ambassador's thought concerning the Home Governments of the five great Powers of Europe was little else than an angry "quos ego!" The sagacious Turks would look more to these great signs than to the tenor of formal advice sent out from London, and if they saw that Lord Stratford was in his heart

* "Eastern Papers," part II. p. 69.

against the opinion of Europe, they would easily resolve to follow his known desire, and to disobey his mere words. The result was that, without any signs of painful doubt, the Turkish Government determined to stand firm. They quietly introduced into the draft the modifications which they deemed to be necessary for extracting its dangerous quality, and resolved that, unless these changes were admitted, they would altogether reject the Note. They were supported by the unanimous decision of the Great Council.

CHAP. XVII.

The Turkish Government determines to reject it unless altered.

It might seem that, with Lord Stratford and the Turkish Government on one side, and all the rest of Europe, including England herself, on the other, the preponderance would be soon determined; and Lord Clarendon remonstrated against the obstinacy of the Turks in terms which approached to a disapproval of all that had lately been done at Constantinople;[*] but Europe was in the wrong, and Lord Stratford and the Turks were in the right; and happily for the world, a strong man and a good cause make a formidable conjunction. Lord Stratford did not fail to show his Government that the objections of the Turks to the proposed Note were well founded; and Europe was compelled to remember that the Russian demand still had in it the original vice of wrongfully seeking to extort a treaty in time of peace.

Lord Stratford and the Turks stand alone in Europe.

On the 19th of August the Porte declined to accept the Vienna Note, without introducing into it

They are firm.

[*] "Eastern Papers," part II. p. 91.

98

CHAP. XVII.

Nesselrode uses language which shows the soundness of Lord Stratford's objection to the Note.

the required alterations.* These alterations were rejected by Russia; and for a moment Europe was threatened with the mortification of seeing that the question of peace or war was to depend upon a mere verbal criticism — and a criticism, too, in which the English Government at first supposed that the Turks were wrong.** It happened, however, that in the course of the discussion, Count Nesselrode argued against the alterations proposed at Constantinople, in language which avowed that the meaning and intent of Russia coincided with that very interpretation which had been fastened upon the Note by the sagacity of the Turks; and the Governments of the four Powers being then obliged to acknowledge that they were wrong, and that Lord Stratford and the Turks were right, the question which brought about the final rupture between Russia and the Porte was virtually the same as that which had caused the departure of Prince Mentschikoff from Constantinople. What Russia still required, and what the Porte still refused to grant, was the Protectorate of the Greek Church in Turkey.

The Protectorate of the Greek Church in Turkey was still the thing in question.

The Porte declares war.

At length, with the advice of a Great Council attended by a hundred and seventy-two of the foremost men of the Empire, the Porte determined upon

---

* "Eastern Papers," part II. p. 80. A copy of the "Vienna Note," and of the alterations insisted upon by the Turks, is given in the Appendix, in order to show the exact difference of words which brought about the final rupture between Russia and the Porte.

** Ibid. p. 91.

war. A declaration was issued, which made the further continuance of peace dependent upon the evacuation of the Principalities; and the Russian General there commanding was summoned to withdraw his troops from the invaded provinces within fifteen days. He did not comply with the demand; and on the 23d of October 1853 the Sultan was placed in a state of war with the Emperor of Russia.

But meanwhile the preachers of the Orthodox Church and the preachers of Islam had not been idle. In Russia, the piety and the spirit of the people had been forestalled by the consuming evil of a vast standing army, and crushed down by police and by drill. The Government had already taken so much by sheer compulsion, that the people, however brave and pious, had little more that it was willing to offer up in sacrifice. It was not thus in the Ottoman Empire. Through the vast and scattered dominions of the Sultan, the holy war had not been preached in vain. There, religion and love of country and warlike ardour were blent into one ennobling sentiment, which was strong enough, as was soon shown, to make men arise of their own free will and endure long toil and cruel hardships that they might attain to some battle-field or siege, and there face death with joy. And under the counsels and ascendancy of Lord Stratford this ardour was so well guided that it was kept from breaking out in vain tumult or outrage, and was brought to bear in all its might upon the defence of the State.

CHAP. XVII.

Modernisation of the Turkish Government.

"A spirit of self-devotion," wrote the Ambassador, "unaccompanied with fanatical demonstrations, and "showing itself amongst the highest functionaries of "the State, bids fair to give an extraordinary impulse "to any military enterprise which may be undertaken "against Russia by the Turkish Government. The "corps of Ulema are preparing to advance a con- "siderable sum in support of the war. The Grand "Vizier, the Minister for Foreign Affairs, and other "leading members of the Administration, have resigned "a large proportion of their horses for the service of "the artillery. Reinforcements continue to be directed "towards the Danube and the Georgian frontier. If "hostilities commence, they will be prosecuted in a "manner to leave, on one side or on the other, deep "and durable traces of a truly national struggle."*

But if the Turkish Empire was still the Caliphate, and if religion still gave the watchword which brought many races of men to crowd to the same standard, yet the Porte, chastened by the adversity of the latter century, and disciplined by the English Ambassador, had become so wise and politic that it governed the beating heart of the nation, and suffered no fanatic words to go out into Christendom. The duty of the Moslem, now called to arms for his Faith, was preached with a fervour sufficing for all military purposes; but the Proclamation which announced that the Sultan was at war abstained from all fierce theo-

* "Eastern Papers," part ii. p 167.

logy. Reiterating the poignant truths which placed the Porte in the right and the Czar in the wrong, it kept to that tone of moderation which had hitherto marked all the State Papers of the Turkish Government. But this very moderation seemed always to kindle fresh rage in the mind of the Emperor Nicholas, and to fetch out his religious zeal. The reason perhaps was, that in all wisdom and all moderation evinced by the Divan he persisted in seeing the evil hand of Lord Stratford. In his Proclamation he ascended to ecstatic heights:— "By the grace of God, "We, Nicholas I., Emperor and Autocrat of All the "Russias, make known: By our Manifesto of the "14th of June, we acquainted our well-beloved and "faithful subjects with the motives which have com- "pelled us to demand of the Ottoman Porte invio- "lable guarantees in favour of the sacred rights of "the Orthodox Church. . . . Russia is challenged to "the fight; nothing, therefore, further remains for "her but, in confident reliance upon God, to have "recourse to arms, in order to compel the Ottoman "Government to respect treaties, and obtain from it "reparation for the offences by which it has respond- "ed to our most moderate demands, and to our le- "gitimate solicitude for the defence of the Orthodox "faith in the East, which is equally professed by "the Russian people. We are firmly convinced that "our faithful subjects will join the fervent prayers "which we address to the Most High, that His hand

CHAP. XVII.

Its effect on the mind of the Czar.

The Czar's Proclamation.

"may be pleased to bless our arms in the holy and "just cause which has ever found ardent defenders "in our pious ancestors. 'In Thee, O Lord, have I "'trusted; let me not be confounded for ever!'"*

* "Eastern Papers," part ii. p. 229.

CHAPTER XVIII.

The Emperor Nicholas still sought to prolong the ambiguity of his relations with Turkey. On the 31st of October, Count Nesselrode issued a Circular to the representatives of Russia at foreign Courts, in which he declared that, notwithstanding the declaration of war, and as long as his master's dignity and his interests would permit, Russia would abstain from taking the offensive, and content herself with holding her position in the Principalities until she succeeded in obtaining the satisfaction which she required. This second endeavour to contrive a novel kind of standing-ground between real peace and avowed war was destined, as will be seen, to cause fresh discord between Russia and the Western Powers.

CHAP. XVIII. The Czar announces that unless he shall be further provoked, he will be content to hold his "material" "guarantee," and refrain from taking the offensive.

The negotiations for a settlement were scarcely interrupted, either by the formal declaration of war, or by the hostilities which were commenced on the banks of the Danube; and the Conference of the four Powers represented at Vienna had just agreed to the terms of a collective Note, which seemed to afford a basis for peace, when the English Government gave way to the strenuous urgency of the French

The negotiations are continued, and are ripening towards a settlement, when they are ruined by the Western Powers.

CHAP. XVIII.

Emperor, and consented to a measure which ruined the pending negotiations, and generated a series of events leading straight to a war between Russia and the Western Powers.

Movement at Constantinople.

In the month of September, some weeks before the Sultan's final rupture with the Czar, the pious and warlike ardour then kindled in the Turkish Empire had begun to show itself at Constantinople. A placard, urging the Government to declare war, was pasted on one of the mosques. Then a petition for war was presented to the Council, and to the Sultan himself, by certain muderris, or theological students. The paper was signed by thirty-five persons of no individual distinction, but having the corporate importance of belonging to the "Ulemah." Though free from menace, the petition, as Lord Stratford expressed it, was worded in "serious and impressive "terms, implying a strong sense of religious duty, and "a very independent disregard of consequences." The Ministers professed to be alarmed, and to believe that this movement was the forerunner of revolution; and Lord Stratford seems to have imagined that their

The use made of this by the Turkish Ministers.

alarm was genuine. It is perhaps more likely that they were skilfully making the most of these occurrences, with a view to embroil their maritime allies in the approaching war; for when they went to the Ambassadors, and asked them to take part in measures for the maintenance of public tranquillity, their meaning was that they wished to see the fleets of France and England come up into the Bosphorus;

and they well knew that if this naval movement could be brought to pass before the day of the final rupture between Russia and the Porte, it would be regarded by the Czar as a flagrant violation of treaty.

A curious indication of the sagacity with which the Turkish Ministers were acting is to be found in the difference between their language to the English Ambassador and their language to M. de la Cour. In speaking to Lord Stratford, they shadowed out dangers impending over the Eastern world, the upheaving of Islam, the overthrow of the Sultan's authority. Then they went straight to M. de la Cour and drew a small vivid picture of massacred Frenchmen. They did not, said M. de la Cour, conceal from him "that the persons and the interests of his countrymen "would be exposed to grave dangers, which they "were sensible they were incapable of preventing, by "reason of the want of union in the Ministry and the "threats directed against themselves."* This skilful discrimination on the part of the Turkish Ministers seems to show that they had not at all lost their composure.

Either by their real dread, or by their crafty simulation of it, the Turkish statesmen succeeded in infecting M. de la Cour with sincere alarm. He was easily brought to the conclusion that "the state of "the Turkish Government was getting worse and "worse; and that matters had got to such a state as

They succeed in alarming the French Ambassador.

---

* "Eastern Papers," part ii. p. 115.

CHAP. XVIII.

"to cause dread of a catastrophe, of which the inhabitants, Rayahs or Europeans, would be the first victims, and which would even threaten the Sultan's throne."* He called upon the English Ambassador to consult as to what was best to be done; and both he and the Austrian Internuncio expressed their readiness to join with him in adopting the needful measures.

Composure of Lord Stratford.

Lord Stratford does not seem to have suspected that the use which the Turkish Ministers were making of their divinity students was in the nature of a stratagem; but, assuming and believing their alarm to be genuine, he was still proof against the infection, and retained his calm. Indeed, he seems to have understood that a cry for war on the part of the religious authorities was a healthy sign for the Empire. He expressed to his colleagues his readiness to act in concert with them; but he said he was reluctant to take any step which was not clearly warranted by the necessities of the case, and that he desired to guard against mistake and exaggeration by gaining a more precise knowledge of the grounds for alarm. He deprecated any joint interference with the Turkish Government, and was still less inclined to join in bringing up the squadrons to Constantinople without more proofs of urgent peril than had been yet obtained; but he suggested, as an opinion of his own, that the representatives of the

His wise and guarded measures for pro-

---

* "Eastern Papers," part II. p. 115.

maritime Powers should obtain from their respective Admirals such an addition of steam-force as would secure them from any immediate attack, and enable them to assist the Government in case of an outbreak threatening its existence, without attracting any unusual attention, or assuming an air of intimidation.* This was done.** A couple of steamers belonging to each of the great Western Powers quietly came up to Constantinople. Tranquillity followed. Every good end was attained without ostentation or disturbance—without the evil of seeming to place the Sultan's capital under the protection of foreign Powers—and, above all, without breaking through the treaty of 1841 in a way which, however justifiable it might be in point of international law, clearly tended to force on a war.

But the moderate and guarded policy of Lord Stratford at Constantinople was quickly subverted by a pressure which the French Emperor found means of putting upon the advisers of the Queen. Of course an understanding with a foreign Power is in its nature an abatement of a nation's free agency; and a statesman may be honest and wise in consenting to measures which have no other excuse than that they were adopted for the sake of maintaining close union with an ally. England had

---

* The steam-force of the maritime Powers already in the Golden Horn consisted of vessels which had passed the Dardanelles by virtue of exceptions contained in the treaty of 1841.

** "Eastern Papers," part ii. p. 121.

contracted a virtual alliance; and when once she had taken this step, it was needful and right that she should do and suffer many things rather than allow the new friendship to be chilled. But this yoke was pressed hard against her. It was not the wont of England to be causelessly led into an action which was violent, and provoking of violence. It was not her wont to rush forward without need, and so to drive through a treaty that many might say she broke it. It was not her wont to be governed in the use of her fleets by the will of a foreign Sovereign. It was not her wont to hear from a French Ambassador that a given movement of her Mediterranean squadron was "indispensably neces-"sary," nor to be requested to go to such a conclusion by "an immediate decision." It was not her wont to act with impassioned haste, where haste was dangerous and needless. It was not her wont to found a breach with one of the foremost Powers of Europe upon a mere hysterical message addressed by one Frenchman to another. But the French Emperor had a great ascendant over the English Government; for the power which he had gained by entangling it in a virtual alliance was augmented by the growing desire for action now evinced by the English people. He knew that at any moment he could expose Lord Aberdeen and his colleagues to a gust of popular disfavour, by causing it to be known or imagined that France was keen, and that England was lagging behind.

When M. de la Cour's account of his sensations reached Paris, it produced so deep an impression that the French Emperor, either feeling genuine alarm, or else seeing in his Ambassador's narrative an opportunity for the furtherance of his designs, determined to insist, in cogent terms, that the English Government should join him in overstepping the treaty of 1841, and ordering the Allied squadrons to pass the Dardanelles and anchor in the Bosphorus. On the 23d of September, Count Walewski had an interview with Lord Aberdeen and Lord Clarendon at the same time; and then, after speaking of the crisis at Constantinople which M. de la Cour's despatch had led the French Government to expect, he said that his Government thought it "indispensably "necessary that both fleets should be ordered up to "Constantinople;" and his Excellency added "that "he was directed to ask for the immediate decision "of Her Majesty's Government, in order that no "time might be lost in sending instructions to the "Ambassadors and Admirals."*

CHAP. XVIII.

Violent urgency of the French Emperor for an advance of the fleets to Constantinople.

Now, at the time of listening to these peremptory words, the English Government had received no account from their own Ambassador of the apprehended disturbances; but they knew that the fleets at the mouth of the Dardanelles, being already under orders to obey the requisitions of the Ambassadors, could be instantly brought up to Constanti-

Needlessness of the measure.

---

* "Eastern Papers," part II. p. 114.

nople without any further orders for that purpose being sent from home. Moreover, the very despatch which brought the alarm showed that the Ambassadors knew how to meet the danger, and that they had already called up that portion of the fleet which they deemed it prudent to have in the Golden Horn. From first to last the power which France and England had intrusted to their representatives at the Porte had been used with admirable prudence; and it is hard to understand how it could have seemed right to withdraw, or rather supersede, the discretion hitherto committed to the Ambassadors, by sending out an absolute order for the advance of the fleets. As it stood, the fleets would go up the moment they were wanted; and what the French Emperor now required was that, whether they were wanted or not, and in defiance of the treaty of 1841, they should immediately pass the Dardanelles. Either the Queen's Government had lost its composure, or else, when they gave way to this demand of the French Emperor, and consented to a needless* measure which operated as a sharp provocative of war, the Queen's Government went through the bitter duty of taking a step not right in itself, but forced upon them by the stringency of the new alliance.

"I told Count Walewski," says Lord Clarendon, "that no intelligence of the nature referred to by M.

---

* Needless, because the authority to call up the fleets when they were wanted was already vested in the Ambassadors.

"de la Cour had been received from Lord Stratford
"de Redcliffe; and that so long as the Porte did not
"declare war against Russia, and desire the presence
"of the British fleet, it was the intention of Her
"Majesty's Government to observe the treaty of 1841;
"but Lord Aberdeen and I concurred in stating to
"Count Walewski that, under such circumstances as
"those reported by M. de la Cour, the provisions of
"any treaty must necessarily, and as a matter of
"course, be set aside." And then, unhappily, Lord
Aberdeen and Lord Clarendon went on to tell Count
Walewski "that they would without hesitation take
"upon themselves to agree to the proposal of the
"French Government that the Ambassadors should
"be instructed to call up the fleets to Constantinople
"for the security of British and French interests, and,
"if necessary, for the protection of the Sultan."*

The English Government yields to the French Emperor.

In compliance with the promise thus obtained from him, Lord Clarendon on the same day addressed a despatch to Lord Stratford, saying, "Your Excel-"lency is therefore instructed to send for the British "fleet to Constantinople"**— thus depriving the Ambassador of the discretion which had hitherto been used with singular care and wisdom, and with great advantage to the public service. What makes the course of the English Government the more extraordinary is, that they rushed into the hostile policy

Fleet ordered up to Constantinople.

Want of firmness and discretion

---

* "Eastern Papers," part II. p. 114.
** Ibid. p. 116.

CHAP. XVIII.
evinced in the adoption of the measure.

which is involved in this stringent order to Lord Stratford without having received any despatch of their own from Constantinople, and without any knowledge of the events which had been there occurring except what was conveyed by a telegraphic message from a French Ambassador to his own Government. If the English Ministers had paused five days,* they would have received Lord Stratford's calm despatch, showing that he looked with more pleasure than alarm upon the petition of the theological students, and that he knew how to avail himself of force without using violence. If they had waited four days more,** they would have found that the hour was at hand when the fleets might enter the Dardanelles without any violation or seeming violation of treaty; and, in fact, it happened that this ill-omened order for the entry of the squadrons into the Dardanelles was carried into effect at a moment when a delay of less than twenty-four hours would have made their entry clearly consistent with a due observance of the treaty of 1841; for they entered the Dardanelles on the 22d, and on the following day the Sultan, being then at war with Russia, was released from the engagement which precluded him (so long as he was at peace) from suffering foreign fleets to come up through the Straits.

Baron Brunnow's remonstrance.

Baron Brunnow remonstrated in strong terms

* i. e., till 28th September. Ibid. p. 121.
** i. e., till 2d October. "Eastern Papers," part II. p. 127.

against the entry of the fleets into the Dardanelles as a breach of the treaty of 1841; and although he was well answered by Lord Clarendon so far as concerned the mere question of right, no endeavour was made to mitigate by words the true import of the measure; and, in truth, it was of so hostile a nature as not to be susceptible of any favourable interpretation; for although the apprehension of disturbances at Constantinople might be a sufficing ground for the step, the order to the Ambassadors was not made dependent upon the occurrence of any such disturbances, nor even upon any alleged fear of them, but was peremptory and absolute in its terms, and was made applicable, not to such a portion of the naval forces as might be requisite for insuring the peace of the city, but to the whole of the Allied squadrons.

CHAP. XVIII.

When the tidings of this hostile measure reached St Petersburg, they put an end for the time to all prospect of peace; and even Count Nesselrode, who had hitherto done all he could venture in the way of resistance to his master, now declared with sorrow that he saw in the acts of the British Government a "settled purpose to humiliate Russia." He spoke in sorrow; and his thoughts, it would seem, went back to the times when he had sat in great councils with Wellington. "He spoke," says Sir Hamilton Seymour, "with much feeling of the horrors of war, and "particularly of war between two powerful countries "— two old allies like England and Russia — countries "which, whilst they might be of infinite use to one

Effect of the measure at St Peters- burg.

Count Nessel- rode's sorrow.

"another, possessed each the means of inflicting great "injury upon its antagonist; and ended by saying "that if, for any motives known to him, war should "be declared against Russia by England, it would "be the most unintelligible and the least justifiable "war ever undertaken."*

<small>The Czar's determination to retaliate with his Black Sea fleet.</small>

The Czar received tidings of the hostile decision of the maritime Powers in a spirit which, this time at least, was almost justified by the provocation given. In retaliation for what he would naturally look upon as a bitter affront, and even as a breach of treaty, he determined, it would seem, to have vengeance at sea whilst vengeance at sea was still possible; and it was under the spur of the anger thus kindled that orders for active operations were given to the fleet at Sebastopol.** The vengeance he meditated he could only wreak upon the body of the Turks, for the great offenders of the West were beyond the bounds of his power.

<small>Error of the notion that the</small>

It was long believed in England that the disaster of Sinope was a surprise stealthily contrived by the

---

* "Eastern Papers," part II. p. 160.

** This conclusion is drawn from dates. The hostile resolution of the Western Powers was known to the Czar a little before the 14th of October, and about the middle of the following month the Black Sea fleet was at sea. If allowance be made for distance and preparation, it will be seen that the sequence of one event upon the other is close enough to warrant the statement contained in the text. In the absence, however, of any knowledge to the contrary, it is fair to suppose that the Czar remembered his promise, and did not sanction any actual attack upon the enemy unless his commanders should be previously apprised that the Turks had commenced active warfare.

Emperor Nicholas, and it is certain that the event fell upon the maritime Powers as a sudden shock; but it is not true that concealment was used by Russia. On the contrary, it seems that the attack was preceded by a long-continued ostentation of naval force. In the middle of the month of November, and at a time when the Allied squadrons were anchored in the Bosphorus, the Sebastopol fleet came out, and was ranged in a kind of cordon stretching from north to south across the centre of the Black Sea. So early as the 20th of November the Russian cruisers captured the Medora, a Turkish steamer;* and about the same time they boarded a merchantman, and relieved the captain of a portion of his cargo and of the whole of his cash;** and the Russians were so far from entertaining any idea of secrecy or concealment, that they seem to have hailed neutral merchantmen for the purpose of inquiring about the French and English fleets in the Bosphorus, and asking "exultingly" if the captures which the Russian fleet had effected were known at Constantinople.*** *CHAP. XVIII. disaster of Sinope was a surprise achieved by stealth.*

Ostentatious publicity of the Russian operations in the Black Sea.

Full ten days† before the fatal 30th of November, a Russian force of seven sail and one war-steamer was cruising in sight of Sinope, and *Tidings of an impending attack by the Russian fleet.*

---
* "Eastern Papers," part ii. p. 315.
** Ibid. p. 316.
*** Ibid. p. 315.
† Ibid. So early as the 22d, the appearance of the squadron was described as having occurred "some days back."

8*

CHAP. XVIII.

hovering over the Turkish squadron which lay there at anchor. An express, despatched from Samsoon by land on the 22d, bore tidings of this to Lord Stratford, and it must have reached him, it would seem, by the 25th or 26th. On Wednesday the 23d, the Commander of the Turkish squadron descried a Russian force of seven sail and two steamers coming down under a north-east wind towards Sinope. The Turkish ships were cleared for action, but after some manœuvring, the Russian force stood out to windward and gained an offing. On the following day six Russian ships of the line, with a brig and two steamers, again made their appearance; and three of them, under easy sail, stood towards the port of Sinope until the evening. "In fine," writes the Turkish Commander, "six sail of the line, a brig, "and two steamers, are constantly off the port above-"mentioned, and at one time they lie-to, and another "they beat about. From six to eight frigates and "two steamers have been seen off the port of Bartin "and Amasbre, and this news is certain. Besides, "the great naval port of the enemy is near. He may "therefore receive reinforcements, or attack us with "fire-ships. That being the case, if reinforcements "are not sent to us, and our position continues the "same for some time — may God preserve us from "them! — it may well happen that the Imperial fleet "may incur disasters."*

* "Eastern Papers," part II. p. 313.

CHAP. XVIII.
Inaction of the Ambassadors and the Admirals.

The power and habit of concentrating all energy in a single channel of action, was one of the qualities which gave force and grandeur to Lord Stratford in the field of diplomacy, but it also seems to have had the effect of preventing him from casting a glance beyond the range of his profession; and it is curious that, when the exigencies of the time called upon him to perform duties not commonly falling within the sphere of a diplomatist, his mind refused to act. England and France, without the wholesome formality of a treaty, had glided into an engagement to defend "Constantinople, or any other part of the "Turkish territory, whether in Europe or in Asia, "that might be in danger of attack."* So much of this grave duty as consisted in originating a resolve to put forth the naval strength of the Allies remained committed to the two Ambassadors, but it was of course understood that any plans for active measures would be concerted between them and the Admirals; and since the nature of the duty which they might be called upon to undertake was known of course to the Admirals, it must be adjudged that it was incumbent upon them, as well as upon the two Ambassadors, to take measures for ascertaining whether the Russians were preparing to operate against the coasts of Turkey. Moreover, the English Ambassador had been instructed by his Government that, "if the Russian fleet were to come out of Sebasto-

---

* "Eastern Papers," part II. p. 143.

"pol, the fleets would then, as a matter of course, "pass through the Bosphorus;"* and, implicitly, this instruction required that measures should be taken for ascertaining whether the Czar's naval forces were in harbour or at sea, for if they were gone to sea, that was an event which (according to the orders from home) was to be the ground of a naval operation.

Yet not only were no measures taken for ascertaining the truth, but the rumours of great naval operations in the Black Sea, and the despatch of the 22d, announcing that the Russian squadron was hovering over Sinope, and even the despatch containing the touching appeal of the Turkish Commander at Sinope, all alike failed to draw men into action. This last despatch was communicated to Lord Stratford on the 29th. Even then an instant advance of the steam squadrons might not have been altogether in vain, for though the attack commenced on the 30th, the Russian fleet did not quit Sinope until the 1st of December. Yet nothing was done. Nothing but actual intelligence of the disaster was cogent enough to lift an anchor. What Lord Stratford says of the causes of all this inaction ought to be stated in his own words. Writing on the 4th of December, he says: "Rumours of Russian ships of "the line being at sea have occasionally prevailed "for some time. Uncertainty of information, a wish

---

* "Eastern Papers," part II. p. 148.

"to avoid as long as possible the chances of a col- CHAP. XVIII.
"lision, the arrival of a new French Ambassador,
"and the state of the weather, were natural causes
"of demur in coming to a decision as to sending
"the squadrons into the Black Sea at this time of
"the year."* But even supposing that there were
reasons which justified hesitation in sending the
squadrons to sea, the Home Governments of the
Western Powers were entitled to ask why some
humbler means of ascertaining the truth were never
resorted to, and why no measures followed upon
the receipt of the alarming despatch from Samsoon,
or even upon the appeal for help which had come
from the Turkish Commander at Sinope.

On the 30th of November, Admiral Nachimoff, The disaster of Sinope.
with six sail of the line, bore down upon the Turkish
squadron still lying at anchor in the port of Sinope.
There was no ship of the line in the Turkish squadron.
It consisted of seven frigates, a sloop, a steamer, and
some transports. The Turks were the first to fire,
and to bring upon their little squadron of frigates
the broadsides of six sail of the line; and although
they fought without hope, they were steadfast. Either
they refused to strike their colours, or else, if their
colours went down, the Russian Admiral was blind
to their signal, and continued to slaughter them.
Except the steamer, every one of the Turkish vessels

* "Eastern Papers," part II. p. 811.

was destroyed. It was believed by men in authority that 4000 Turks were killed, that less than 400 survived, and that all these were wounded.* The feeble batteries of the place suffered under the enemy's fire, and the town was much shattered.* The Russian fleet did not move from Sinope until the following day.*

This onslaught upon Sinope, and upon vessels lying in port, was an attack upon Turkish territory, and was therefore an attack which the French and English Ambassadors had been authorised to repel by calling into action the fleets of the Western Powers. Moreover, this attack had been impending for many days, and all this while the fleets of the Western Powers had been lying still in the Bosphorus within easy reach of the scene of the disaster. The honour of France was wounded. England was touched to the quick.

* "Eastern Papers," part II. p. 305.

CHAPTER XIX.

EITHER from sheer want of forethought, or else in tenderness to the feelings of men who shunned the bare thought of a collision, the Governments of France and England had omitted to consider the plight in which they would stand, if, under the eyes of their naval commanders, a Russian Admiral should come out from Sebastopol and crush a Turkish squadron in the midst of the Black Sea. It is true that this was not the event which had occurred, for the onslaught of Sinope was "an attack upon Tur-"kish territory," and was therefore within the scope of the instructions from home. But it is also true that the Governments of Paris and London had not committed, either to their Ambassadors or their Admirals, any power to take part in a naval engagement against Russia upon the open sea; and it was obvious that this chasm in the instructions furnished a ground of palliation to the Ambassadors and the naval commanders; for, after all the angry negotiations that had taken place between Russia and the Western Powers, a French or an English Admiral

CHAP. XIX. Chasm in the instructions furnished to the Admirals of the Western Powers.

might naturally be loth to go watching the movements of a fleet which, so long as it was upon the open sea, he was not empowered to strike, and might be honourably reluctant to move out into the Euxine and run the risk of having to witness a naval engagement between the ships of the Czar and of the Sultan, without being at liberty to take part in it unless it chanced to be fought within gunshot of the Turkish coast. But exactly in proportion as this excuse for the Ambassadors and Admirals was valid, it tended to bring blame upon the Home Governments of France and England. The honest rage of the English people was about to break out, and there were materials for a rough criticism of men engaged in the service of the State. Some might blame the Home Government, some the Ambassador, some the Admiral; but plainly it would fare ill with any man upon whom the public anger might light.

On the 11th of December the tidings of Sinope reached Paris and London. The French Government felt the bitterness of a disaster "endured as it "were under the guns of the French and English "fleets."* In England the indignation of the people ran to a height importing a resolve to have vengeance; and if it had clearly been understood that the disaster had resulted from a want of firm orders

---

* M. Drouyn de Lhuys. "Eastern Papers," part II. p. 239.

from home, the Government would have been overwhelmed. But the very weight and force of the public anger gave the Government a means of eluding it. The torrent had so great a volume that it was worthy to be turned against a foreign State. The blaming of Ministers and Ambassadors and Admirals, and the endless conflict which would be engendered by the apportionment of censure, all might be superseded by suggesting, instead, a demand for vengeance against Russia. The terms of Count Nesselrode's Circular of the 31st of October * had given ground for expecting that, until provoked to a contrary course, the Czar, notwithstanding the Turkish declaration of war, would remain upon the defensive; and the people in England were now taught, or allowed to suppose, that Russia had made this attack upon a Turkish squadron in breach of an honourable understanding virtually equivalent to a truce, or, at all events, to an arrangement which would confine the theatre of active war to the valley of the Lower Danube. This charge against Russia was unjust; for after the issue of the Circular, the Government of St Petersburg had received intelligence not only that active warfare was going on in the valley of the Lower Danube, but that the Turks had seized the Russian fort of St Nicholas, on the eastern coast of the Euxine, and were attacking

CHAP. XIX.

The anger of the English people is diverted from official personages and brought to bear on the Czar.

An unjust charge against the Czar gains full belief in England.

* See ante.

Russia upon her Armenian frontier. After acts of this warlike sort had been done, it was impossible to say, with any fairness, that Russia was debarred from a right to destroy her enemy's ships; and it must be acknowledged also, as I have already said, that the destruction of the Turkish squadron at Sinope was not a thing done in stealth. But the people of England, not knowing all this at first, and hearing nothing of the Russian fleet until they heard of the ravage and slaughter of Sinope, imagined that the blow had come sudden as the knife of an assassin. They were too angry to be able to look upon the question in a spirit of cold justice. It was therefore an easy task to turn all attention from the faults of public functionaries and fasten it upon a larger scheme of vengeance. Ministers, Ambassadors, and Admirals, went free, and in a spirit of honest, inaccurate justice, the Emperor Nicholas was marked for sacrifice. This time it was his fate to be condemned on wrong grounds; but his sins against Europe had been grievous, and the rough dispensations of the tribunal which people call "opinion" have often enough determined that a man who has been guilty of one crime shall be made to suffer for another. There were few men in England who doubted that the onslaught of Sinope was a treacherous deed.

First decision of the English

When the Cabinet met to consult upon the questions raised by the tidings from Sinope, it came to the conclusion that the fleets of the Western Powers would forthwith enter the Euxine; and the majority were of opinion that the instructions addressed to the English Admiral on the 8th of October, reinforced by a warning that such a disaster as Sinope must not be repeated, would be still a sufficing guide. But Lord Palmerston saw that, even if this resolution was suited to the condition of things on the shores of the Bosphorus, it would find no mercy at home. In truth he was gifted with the instinct which enables a man to read the heart of a nation. He saw, he felt, he knew that the English people would never endure to hear of the disaster of Sinope, and yet be told that nothing was done. He resigned his office. The residuum of the Cabinet determined to leave the English Admiral under the guidance of his own instructions.

<small>CHAP. XIX.
Cabinet in regard to Sinope.</small>

<small>Lord Palmerston resigns office.</small>

But on the 16th of December the Emperor of the French once more approached the Government of the Queen with his subtle and dangerous counsels. The armed conflict of States in these times is an evil of such dread proportions that it seems wise to uphold the solemnity of a transition from peace to war, and to avoid those contrivances which tend to throw down the great landmark; for experience shows that statesmen heartily resolved upon peace may nevertheless be induced to concur in a series of gentle steps which slowly and gradually lead down to war. The negotiations for a settlement between

<small>Proposal of the French Emperor.</small>

<small>Danger of breaking down the old barriers between peace and war.</small>

CHAP. XIX.

Russia and Turkey had not only been revived, but were far from being at this time in an unpromising state; and it is probable that if Lord Aberdeen and Mr Gladstone had been called upon to say whether they would observe peace faithfully, or frankly declare a war, they would scarcely have made the more violent choice. But the alternative was not presented to the minds of the Queen's Ministers in this plain and wholesome form.

Ambiguous character of the proposal.

The ingenious Emperor of the French devised a scheme of action so ambiguous in its nature that, at the option of any man who spoke about it, it might be called either peace or war, but so certain nevertheless, in its tendency, that the adoption of it by the maritime Powers would blot out all fair prospect of maintaining peace in Europe. He proposed to give Russia notice "that France and Eng-"land were resolved to prevent the repetition of the "affair of Sinope, and that every Russian ship "thenceforward met in the Euxine would be re-"quested, and, if necessary, constrained, to return to "Sebastopol; and that any act of aggression after-"wards attempted against the Ottoman territory or "flag would be repelled by force."* This proposal involved, without expressing it, a defensive alliance with Turkey against Russia; and, if it were adopted, the Emperor of Russia would have to see his flag

* "Eastern Papers," part ii. p. 307.

driven from the waters which bounded his own dominions. It was so framed that Lord Palmerston would know it meant war, whilst Lord Aberdeen and Mr Gladstone might be led to imagine that it was a measure rather gentle than otherwise, which perhaps would keep peace in the Euxine. Indeed, the proposal seemed made to win the Chancellor of the Exchequer; for it fell short of war by a measure of distance which, though it might seem very small to people with common eyesight, was more than broad enough to afford commodious standing-room to a man delighting as he did in refinements and slender distinctions.

The Emperor of the French pressed this scheme upon the English Cabinet with his whole force. He not only urged it by means of the usual channels of diplomatic communication, but privately desired Lord Cowley "to recommend it in the strongest "terms to the favourable attention of Her Majesty's "Government as a measure incumbent upon himself "and them to take;" and he avowed "the disappoint- "ment which he should feel if a difference of opinion "prevented its adoption."* This language is cogent -- it is also significant; and, to one who can read it by the light of a little collateral knowledge, it may open a glimpse of the relations subsisting between the French Court and public men in England.

* "Eastern Papers," part II. p. 307.

CHAP. XIX.

Lord Aberdeen's Cabinet yields, and adopts, with a slight addition, the French Emperor's scheme.

On the 17th the English Government had taken a step in pursuance of the decision to which the majority of the Cabinet had come; but on the following day they were made acquainted with the will of the French Emperor. It would seem that there was a struggle in the Cabinet; but by the 24th all resistance had broken down, and the first decision of the Government was overturned. The proposal of the French Emperor closed in like a net round the variegated group which composed Lord Aberdeen's Ministry, and gathered them all together in its supple folds. Some submitted to it for one reason, and some for another; but the pressure of the French Emperor was the cogent motive which governed the result. Still, this time, though the pressure was inflicted by the hand of a foreign sovereign, it was after all from the English people themselves that the French Emperor drew his strongest means of coercion. Their indignation at the disaster of Sinope made him sure that he could bring ruin on Lord Aberdeen's Administration by merely causing England to know that her Government was shrinking from the hostile scheme of action which he had proposed.

The result, however, was that now, for the second time, France dictated to England the use that she should make of her fleet, and by this time perhaps submission had become more easy than it was at first. The Ministry, with much openness, acknowledged that they were acting without the warrant of their own judgment, and in deference to the will of the French Emperor. "The Government," said Lord Clarendon, "having announced that the recurrence of "a disaster such as that at Sinope must be prevented, "and that the command of the Black Sea must be "secured, would have been content to have left the "manner of executing those instructions to the dis- "cretion of the Admirals, but they attach so much "importance not alone to the united action of the "two Governments, but to the instructions addressed "to their respective agents being precisely the same, "that they are prepared to adopt the specific mode "of action now proposed by the Government of the "Emperor."* This being resolved, Lord Palmerston consented to return to office.** With the addition of a proviso that for the present the Sultan should be engaged to abstain from aggressive operations on the Euxine, instructions exactly in accord with the French Emperor's proposal were forthwith sent out to the Bosphorus, and at the same time the French

CHAP. XIX.

Lord Palmerston withdraws his resignation.

Orders to execute the scheme and to announce it at St Petersburg.

---

* "Eastern Papers," part II. p. 331.

** His secession during these ten or twelve days was afterwards stated by him to have been based upon a question of home politics, but it would not, of course, follow from this statement that no other motives were governing him; and when it is remembered that his resignation was simultaneous with the first resolution of the Cabinet, and that his return to office coincided with the Cabinet's adoption of the French Emperor's scheme, it will hardly be questioned that the four events may be fairly enough placed in an order which suggests the relation of cause and effect.

CHAP. XIX. and English representatives at St Petersburg were ordered to communicate this resolution to Count Nesselrode.

CHAPTER XX.

AFTER much labour, the representatives of the four Powers at Constantinople had agreed upon a scheme of settlement which they deemed likely to be acceptable to the Emperor Nicholas, and they pressed its adoption by the Porte. The warlike spirit of the Ottoman people had been rising day by day, and it became very hard and dangerous for the Government to venture upon entertaining a negotiation for peace. But Lord Stratford had power over the minds of Turkish Statesmen; and he exerted it with so great a force that, although it was now impossible for them to obey him without having to face a religious insurrection, they obeyed him nevertheless. The fury of the armed divines, insisting upon the massacre of worldlings, was less terrible to them than the anger of the Eltchi. To his will they bent. Not only the Turkish Cabinet, but even the Great Council of State, was brought to accept the terms proposed.* The difficulty, nay the peril of

CHAP. XX. Terms of settlement agreed to by the four Powers, and forced upon the acceptance of the Turks by Lord Stratford.

---

* The terms were finally accepted on the 31st of December 1853. "Eastern Papers," part II. p 362.

CHAP. XX.

Grounds for expecting an amicable solution.

life, which had thus been encountered by the Turkish Ministry for the sake of making peace with Russia — the success achieved at Sinope — and some victories gained over the Turks on the Armenian frontier, — all these were circumstances tending to assuage the mortification inflicted upon the Czar by the failure of Prince Mentschikoff's mission. Again, it had long been plain that the time was ill-fitted for the promotion of any scheme of Russian ambition; and it was known that the English Ambassador had brought the Turks to the utmost verge of possible concession. Moreover, terms of arrangement, agreed to by the Turkish Government, were about to be pressed upon the Czar with all the authority of the four great Powers. It might seem, therefore, that all things were conducing towards an amicable settlement. Nor was this hope at all shaken when the Government of St Petersburg was made acquainted with the first and unbiassed decision to which the English Government had come after hearing of the disasters of Sinope. Apprised by his private letters of the tenor of this decision, Sir Hamilton Seymour gathered or inferred that the Admirals of the Western Powers, being enjoined to prevent the recurrence of an attack like the attack of Sinope, would assert the command of the Black Sea; and when he imparted to the Russian Government the impression thus produced on his mind, his communication was received in a wise and friendly

Friendly reception by the Russian Govern-

spirit by Count Nesselrode; for after hearing that the Western Powers would be likely to assume the command of the Black Sea, the Count "expressed his "belief that the Russian fleet would, in consequence "of the advanced season, be little likely to leave "Sebastopol;" and he then went on to suggest that, if the Russians were to be hindered from attacking the Turks, it would be fair that the Turks should be restrained from molesting the coast of Russia. The rest of the conversation related to the pending negotiations; and, upon the whole, it was plain that the first decision of the English Cabinet was looked upon as the natural result of the engagement at Sinope, that it would certainly not lead to a rupture,* and that at length the Russian Government was in a fit temper to receive the proposals for peace which the four Powers (with the concurrence this time of Lord Stratford, and with the extorted assent of the Turks) were now again bringing to St Petersburg. But whilst this fair prospect was opened by the unceasing toil of the negotiators, there were messengers then journeying from Paris and from London to the Court of St Petersburg; and they carried an announcement that the Western Powers were resolved to execute the harsh and insulting scheme of action which had been forced upon the acceptance of Lord Aberdeen's Cabinet by the Em-

CHAP. XX. ment of the news of the first decision of the English Cabinet.

Announcement at St Petersburg of the scheme finally adopted by the Western Powers.

---

* "Eastern Papers," part ii. p. 859.

CHAP. XX.

peror of the French. Of course it was not to be expected that the friendly spirit in which the Russian Government had received the first and unbiassed decision of the English Cabinet would even for one moment survive an announcement of the scheme which only some ten days later our Government had been brought to adopt. It was one thing for the Western Powers to enforce the neutrality of the Black Sea, and another and a very different thing to announce to the sovereign of a haughty State that, even although he might be bent on no warlike errand, still, upon the very sea which washed his coast — upon the very sea which filled his harbours — he was forbidden to show his flag.

On the 12th of January 1854, the Emperor Nicholas was forced to hear — to endure to hear — that, upon peril of an unequal conflict with the combined fleets of the Western Powers, every ship that he had in the Euxine must either be kept from going to sea, or else must sail by stealth, and be liable to be ignominiously driven back into port.

The negotiations are ruined. The negotiation, which had seemed to be almost ripe for a settlement, was then ruined. The Emperor Nicholas did not declare war against the Western Powers; but, as soon as he received the hostile announcement in a form which he deemed to be official, he withdrew his representatives from Paris and London. The Governments of France and England followed his example; and on the 21st

Rupture of diplomatic relations.

of February 1854, the diplomatic relations between Russia and the Western Powers were brought to a close. Moreover, the Czar prepared to undertake an invasion of the Ottoman dominions.

<small>CHAP XX.

The Czar prepares to invade Turkey.</small>

On the 4th of January 1854, the fleets of England and France moved up and entered the Euxine. <small>Fleets enter the Euxine.</small>

CHAPTER XXI.

Military error of the Czar in occupying Wallachia.

IN a military point of view, and upon the supposition of there being no understanding between Russia and Austria, the seizure of the whole of Wallachia by a Russian army is a dangerous measure; for, after reaching Bucharest, the line of occupation has to bend at right angles, ascending the northern bank of the Danube between an enemy expectant and an enemy already declared, till at length it touches the frontier of the Banat, at a distance from Moscow of not less than a thousand miles. To be in fitting strength at a point thus situate would imply the possession of resources beyond those which Russia could command.

Of this Omar Pasha takes skilful advantage.

The General at the head of the Turkish army was Omar Pasha; and it chanced that he was a man highly skilled in the art of bringing political views to bear upon the operations of an army in the field. He knew that, in protruding his forces into Lesser Wallachia, the Emperor Nicholas was committing a military fault; and he also inferred that political reasons and imperial vanity would make the Czar

PLATE N°

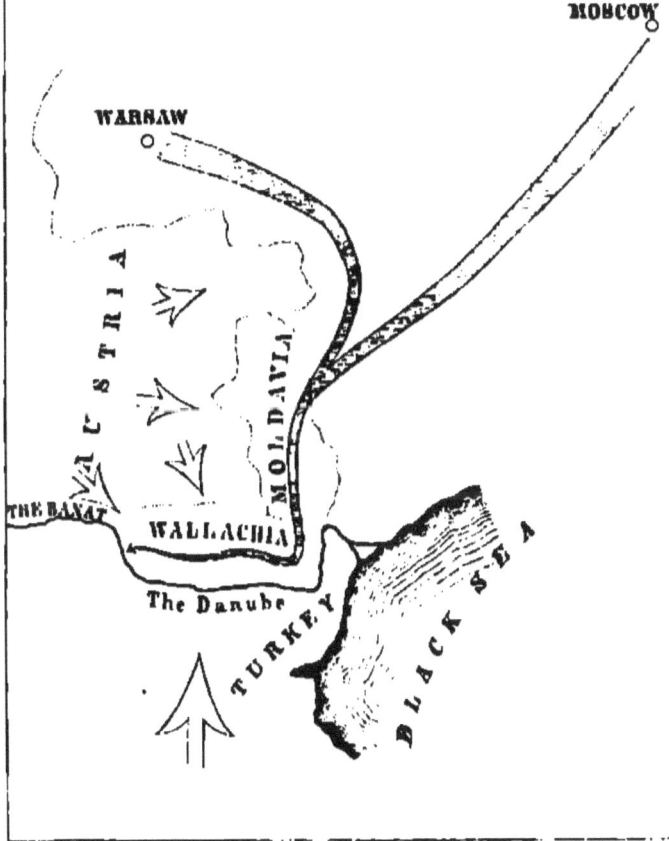

Diagram indicating the nature of the straits in which the Czar placed himself by attempting to maintain a hostile occupation of the Danubian Principalities without the assent of Austria.

The tapering of the lines which shew the route of the Czar's intruding forces is intended to remind the reader of the hourly decreasing strength of an invader who operates at a vast distance from his main resources.

cling to his error. He also knew that, for the rest of that year, the Czar, being kept back by the engagements which he had taken, by his fear of breaking with the four Powers, and, above all, by the insufficiency of his means, would abstain from any further invasion of Turkey, and would even be reluctant to alarm Europe by allowing the least glimpse of a Russian uniform to appear on the right bank of the Danube. Omar saw that the river had thus become a political barrier which protected the Turks from the Russians, without protecting the Russians from the Turks. He could, therefore, overstep the common rules of the art of war; and, disporting himself as he chose on the line of the Danube, could concentrate forces on his extreme left, without any fear for his centre or his right.

Therefore, in the early part of the autumn, a large portion of the Turkish army was quietly drawn to Widdin, a town on the right bank of the river, in the westernmost angle of Bulgaria; and, on the fifth day from the declaration of war, Omer Pasha was over the Danube, intrenching himself at Kalafat, and so established that he faced towards the east, and confronted the extreme flank of the intruding army.* From that moment Nicholas ceased to be the undisturbed holder of the territory which he had chosen to call his "material guarantee." His pride was touched. Tortured by the thought that his power to

* 28th October 1853. The declaration of war became absolute on the 23d.

CHAP. XXI.

hold the pledge was challenged by a Turkish officer, he began to exhaust his strength in efforts to assemble a force at the westernmost point of his extended flank. This was the error which Omar Pasha wished him to commit. At the close of the year, the Czar had succeeded in pushing a heavy body of troops into Lesser Wallachia; and in the beginning of January the lines of Kalafat were attacked by General Aurep. The struggle lasted four days, but it ended in the retreat of the Russian forces; and considering the vast distance between the lines of Kalafat and the home of the Russian army, it may be inferred that this fruitless effort of imperial pride must have worked a deep cavity in the military strength of the Czar.

Moreover, Omar Pasha took another and a not less skilful advantage of the political considerations which prevented the Russians from passing the Danube; for, during the winter, he fleshed his troops by indulging them with enterprises against the enemy's posts along the whole line of the Lower Danube from Widdin to Rassova; and since these attacks were often attended with success, and could never be signally repressed by an enemy who had precluded himself from the right of crossing the river, they gave the Turks that sense of strength in fight which is at the root of warlike prowess.

Embarrassment and distress of the Czar.

Early in the winter the Emperor Nicholas came to understand the fault which he had committed in prescribing the Danube as a boundary — a boundary to be observed by himself, without the least right for expecting that it would be observed by his adversary. So now he would do the contrary of what he had done. Because he had committed a military fault in forbidding himself from all enterprises against the slowly-assembling forces of the Porte in 1853, he would now, in 1854, undertake an invasion which must bring him into conflict with the gathered strength of the Ottoman Empire, and that, too, when it had become certain that the armed support of France and England would not be wanting to the Sultan. But perhaps, after all, it was hardly tolerable for a haughty monarch to have to stand passive under the insulting coercion which was now to be applied to him by the Western Powers; and the Czar, having no means of hostile action against the territories or the ships of either France or England, could only strike at his greater foes by striking at the ally whom they had undertaken to befriend. Upon the whole, therefore, he could not so school himself as to be able to abstain from attempting an invasion of Turkey; but the wholesome trials which he had now undergone had so far disciplined his spirit that at length, after bitter anguish, he felt and acknowledged to himself the want of a firm adviser.

CHAP. XXI.

Russia owned a great General who had never sanctioned by his counsel the errors of the previous year; and now — baffled — agitated — driven hither and thither by alternating impulses till his brain

He resorts for aid to Paskievitch.

CHAP. XXI.

Paskievitch's counsels.

had become a guide more blind than chance — the Czar abated his personal claims to the conduct of a war, and came for help and counsel to the veteran Paskievitch. The evil was almost beyond the old man's hope of cure; for how could Russia march upon Constantinople — nay, how in strict prudence could she march upon the Balkan whilst England and France were in full command of the Euxine? But was the Czar then simply powerless against Turkey? Had his million of soldiers been torn from their homes in vain? Had he not busied himself all his days in organising armies and reviewing drilled men, and grinding down his people into the mere fractional components of an army, until the very faces of soldiers in the same battalion were brought to be similar and uniform? Had his life been utter foolishness, and was the labour of his reign so barren that he could not now make a campaign against the simple Turks, who never took pains about anything until the hour of battle? Had he not spoken in the councils of Europe as though he were a potentate so great that the Empire of the Ottomans existed by force of his magnanimity? And now, had it come to this, that at the mere bidding of the Western Powers, and without their firing a shot, he was to stand arrested in the presence of scoffing Europe like a prisoner who had delivered his sword?

Well, Paskievitch, in a painful, soldierly way, could tell him what would be the least imprudent plan for attacking the inner dominions of the Sultan.

The principles of the art of war have a great stability; CHAP. XXI.
and although there is an infinite variety in the
methods of applying them, it results that the invasion of one nation by another is repeatedly undertaken upon the same accustomed route.

By the route which Paskievitch recommended, the invader crosses the Danube in the neighbourhood of its great bend towards the north; makes himself master of Silistria; encounters and overcomes the assembled strength of the Ottoman Empire in front of the great intrenched camp of Shoumla; then, advancing, forces the difficult passes of the Balkan as best he may; marches upon Adrianople; and thence on — thence on, if he can and dares — to the shore of the Bosphorus. Erivanski* could hardly have believed that his master's military power was equal to so great an undertaking as that; but if it succeeded only in some of its early stages, diplomacy might come to the rescue of the Czar, as it had done in 1829; and the plan had this in its favour, that it placed a broad tract of country between Austria and the right flank of the invading army, and another though less extended territory between its left flank and the fleets of the Western Powers.

But in the counsels of a wise and faithful soldier there is a pitiless candour — a dreadful precision. He comes in his hard way to weights, and to numbers,

* This was Paskievitch's title: it denoted that he was the conqueror of Erivan, a province conquered from the Persians.

CHAP. XXI.

and to measurements of space and of time. Without mercy to the vanity of his suffering master, Paskievitch defaced the cherished form of the "material "guarantee," by insisting that the Czar should cease from trying to hold the Principalities entire, and that all his forces should be quickly withdrawn from the Lesser Wallachia. This done, he promised the Czar an invasion of the Ottoman Empire; but the carrying of the enterprise beyond the valley of the Danube was to be only upon condition that Silistria should fall, and should fall before the 1st of May.*

Movement of troops in the Russian Empire.

So now the streams of battalions rumoured to be setting in upon the Lower Danube from the confines of All the Russias woke up the mind of Europe, and portended a great invasion.

* My knowledge of the counsels tendered to the Emperor by Paskievitch is derived from papers in the possession of the late Lord Raglan.

CHAPTER XXII.

IT has been seen that without treaty, and without the advice or knowledge of Parliament — nay even, perhaps, without a distinct conception of what it was doing — the English Government had been gradually contracting engagements which were almost equivalent to a defensive alliance with the Sultan. France, by virtue of her new understanding with England, had come under the same obligations; and now that an invasion of the Ottoman Empire was threatened, it became necessary that the Western Powers should take measures for its defence. At first, however, their views were limited to the defence of the Sultan's home territories, and especially those which gave the control of the Dardanelles and the Bosphorus. Two Engineer officers — Colonel Ardent on the part of France, and Sir John Burgoyne on the part of England — were despatched to Turkey, with instructions to report upon the best means of aiding the Sultan to defend his home dominions; and almost at the same time it was agreed between the two Western Powers that each of them should prepare to send a small body of troops into the Levant.

CHAP. XXII.

Sir John Burgoyne and Colonel Ardent despatched to the Levant.

CHAP.
XXII.
———
Troops
sent to
Malta.

Tendency
of this
measure.

The English force was collected at Malta. Of the Ministers who joined in adopting this measure, some foresaw that the few battalions which they were despatching to the East were the nucleus of an army which might have to operate in the field; but others looked upon them as a force intended to support our negotiations. This ambiguity of motive was a root of evil; for the collateral arrangements which are requisite for enabling an army to live, to move, and to fight, bear a vast proportion to the mere business of collecting the men; and there is always a danger that a body of troops, sent towards the scene of action with a diplomatic intent, will be unsupported by the measures which are requisite for actual war, and yet, upon the rupture of the negotiations, will be prematurely hurried into the field. On the other hand, the councillors of a great military State are so well accustomed to know the cost and the labour which must precede the advance of an army, that the mere protrusion of a body of well-equipped troops, unsupported by the collateral appliances of war, does not tell upon their minds as a proof of an intention to act. By despatching a few battalions to Malta, without instructing Commissaries to go to the Levant and begin buying up the agricultural wealth of the country, we not only subjected our troops to the danger of their being brought into the field before supplies were ready, but also convinced the Russians that we could not be sincerely intending to engage in a war. Moreover, the slenderness of the addition which the Government proposed to make to our army tended to prolong the Czar's fond confidence in the weight and strength of the English Peace Party; and perhaps this dangerous error was strengthened, if Baron Brunnow was able to tell him that, in proposing to the Cabinet a material increase of our land-forces, the Duke of Newcastle stood almost alone.

CHAP. XXII.
Ministers determine to propose but a small increase of the army.

The Prime Minister's continued persistency in the use of hurtful language was another of the causes which still helped to keep the Czar blindfold. Lord Aberdeen abhorred the bare thought of war; and he would not have suffered his country to be overtaken by it, if the coming danger had been of such a kind that it could be warded off by hating it and shunning its aspect. But it is not by intemperate hatred of war, nor yet by shunning its aspect, that war is averted. Almost to the last, Lord Aberdeen misguided himself. His loathing of war took such a shape that he could not and would not believe in it; and when at last the spectre was close upon him, he covered his eyes and refused to see. Basing himself upon the thoughtless saying of a statesman, who had laid it down that there could be no war in Europe when France and England were agreed, he seems to have imagined that, although he was suffering himself to be drawn on and on into measures which were always becoming less and less short of war, still he could maintain peace by taking care to be always along with the French Emperor; and he

Continuance of Lord Aberdeen's imprudent language.

so clung to the paradise created by a false maxim that he could not be torn from it. He would not be roused from a dream which was sweeter than all waking thoughts; and even now, to any man to whom he chanced to speak, he continued to say that there could not, there would not be war. Coming from a Prime Minister, such words as these did not fail to have a noxious weight with many who heard them. Baron Brunnow, we have seen, had looked deeper even at a much earlier period, and now again, no doubt, he took care to warn his master that Lord Aberdeen was under a passionate hatred of war which deprived him of his competence to speak in the name of his country: but by other channels the words of our Prime Minister were carried to the Emperor of Russia, and, being very welcome to him, and coinciding with his long cherished notions, they tended to keep him in the perilous belief that Lord Aberdeen was speaking with knowledge, and that England, still clogged by her Peace Party, was unable to go to war.

CHAPTER XXIII.

A NEW opportunity of making his way back to peace was now thrown away by the Czar. The exigencies of a throne based upon the deeds of the 2d of December were always driving the French Emperor to endeavour to allay the remembrance of the past by creating a stir in Europe, and endeavouring to win celebrity. When Europe was quiet, he was obliged, for his life's sake, to become its disturber; but when it was at war, or threatened with war, he was willing, it seems, to take an exactly opposite method of attaining the required conspicuousness; for he was not a bloodthirsty nor even a very active-minded man, and there seems no good reason to doubt that, having brought Europe to the state in which it was at the close of January, he was sincere in the pacific step which he then took. At a moment when war was already kindled and seemed to be on the point of involving the great Powers, the odd vanity and the theatric bent which had so strangely governed his life, might easily make him wish to come upon the scene and bestow the blessing of peace upon the grateful, astonished nations. On the other hand, an English Minister would be careless of this kind of celebrity, and, so that peace could be restored to Europe, would be well pleased that the honour of the achievement should seem to belong to the French Emperor.

There is no reason to doubt that the English Government assented to the somewhat startling plan under which the French Emperor conceived himself entitled to speak for the Queen of England as well as for himself; and certainly the licence, however strange it may appear, was in strict consistency with the spirit of the understanding which seems to have been established between the two Western Powers.*

On the 29th of January the French Emperor addressed an autograph letter to his "good friend" of All the Russias. The letter in many parts of it was ably worded, and moderate in its tone, but it was mainly remarkable for the language in which the French Emperor took upon himself to speak and even to threaten war in the name of the Queen of England. After suggesting a scheme of pacification, he said to the Czar: "Let your Majesty adopt this "plan, upon which the Queen of England and myself "are perfectly agreed, and tranquillity will be re- "established and the world satisfied. There is nothing

---

* See the inferred purport of this understanding as stated ante, p. 70, & seq.

"in the plan which is unworthy of your Majesty — "nothing which can wound your honour; but if, from "a motive difficult to understand, your Majesty should "refuse this proposal, then France as well as England "will be compelled to leave to the fate of arms and "the chances of war that which might now be de-"cided by reason and justice."* The French Emperor permitted himself to write this at a time when, so far as is known, no threat like that which he chose to utter in the name of the Queen had been addressed by the English Cabinet to the Court of St Petersburg.

With the feelings which might be expected from them, English Ministers of State have generally been slow to use threatening words; and they have been chary, too, in putting forward the name of their Sovereign. Our Government could not have been willing that England should be thrust upon the attention of the world in a way which the too fastidious Court of St Petersburg would be sure to regard as grotesque. No one can doubt the pain with which the members of Lord Aberdeen's Cabinet must have seen the French Emperor come forward upon the stage of Europe, and publicly menace the Emperor of Russia in the name of their Queen. The process by which they were brought to suffer this is unknown to me. What seems probable is, that a draft of the

* "Annual Register," 1854.

letter was submitted to them, accompanied with significant representations of the importance which the French Emperor attached to it, and that the Cabinet yielded to the pressure because it feared that resistance might chill the new alliance, and might even perhaps cause it to be suddenly abandoned for an alliance between Russia and France.

The letter proposed an armistice, in order to leave open a free course for negotiation. It would seem that, in a military point of view, an armistice for a limited period, commencing in the early days of February, could not have been inconvenient to a Sovereign whose main difficulty at that time lay in the immense marches which he had to effect within his own dominions; and, on the other hand, to any one acquainted with the French Emperor's personal weakness, it was obvious that, by a little harmless play upon his vanity, Russia might hope to obtain a great diplomatic advantage, and to effect a decorous escape from her troubles. But the Czar was not politic; and, instead of seizing the proffered occasion, he not only rejected the overture, but aggravated his refusal by an unwise allusion to the French disasters of 1812.

Mission to St Petersburg from the English Peace Party.

In his quest after this sort of fame the French Emperor was not without rivals. We have seen the share which the English Peace Party had had in misleading the Emperor of Russia, and tempting him to become a disturber by withdrawing the wholesome fear which deters a man from venturing upon outrage. Certain brethren of the Society of Friends, who had been prominent members of this Party, now thought it becoming or wise to proceed to St Petersburg and request the Emperor of All the Russias to concur with them in preserving Europe from the calamity of war.

CHAP. XXIII.

A little later, and the Czar would have stamped in fury and driven from his sight any hapless aide-de-camp who had come to him with a story about a deputation from the English Peace Party; for the hour was at hand when his curses were about to fall heavy on the men who had led him on into all his troubles by pretending that England was immersed in trade, and resolved to engage in no war.* But at this time his hope of seeing our Government held back by the Peace Party had not altogether vanished, and he resolved to give this strange mission a genial welcome.

Of course, the political conversation between the booted Czar and the men of peace was sheer nothingness; but what followed shows the care with which Nicholas had studied the middle classes of England. When he thought that the first scene of the interlude had lasted long enough, he suddenly said to his prim visitors, "By the by, do you know my wife?" They said they did not. The Czar pre-

---

* The scene of violence here prospectively alluded to will be mentioned in a later volume: it occurred in the autumn.

CHAP. XXIII. sented them to the Empress. She charmed them with her kindly grace. They came away sorrowing to think that their wrongheaded countrymen in England should be seeking a quarrel with so good and well-meaning a man as friend Nicholas Romanoff; but perhaps what more than all else laid hold of their hearts, was the thought that the Czar called his Empress so naturally by her dear homely title of wife.

CHAPTER XXIV.

WELCOME or unwelcome, the truth must be told. A huge obstacle to the maintenance of peace in Europe was raised up by the temper of the English people. In public, men still used forms of expression implying they would be content for England to lead a quiet life among the nations, and they still classed expectations of peace amongst their hopes, and declared in joyous tones that the prospects of war were gloomy and painful; but these phrases were the time-honoured canticles of a doctrine already discarded, and they who used them did not mean to deceive their neighbours, and did not deceive themselves. The English desired war; and perhaps it ought to be acknowledged that there were many to whom war, for the sake of war, was no longer a hateful thought. Either the people had changed, or else there was hollowness in some of the professions which orators had made in their name.

When, by lapse of years, the glory of the great war against France had begun to fade from the daily thoughts of the people, they inclined to look more

CHAP. XXIV. Temper of the English an obstacle to the maintenance of peace.

Their desire for war.

Causes of the apparent change in their feeling.

narrowly than before into the origin of taxes, and were not unwilling to hear that their burthens were the result of wars which might have been easily avoided. Moreover, it chanced that from after Marlborough's time downwards, or, at all events, from after the period of Chatham's ascendancy, the wars in which England found herself engaged had been originated and conducted for the most part under the auspices of the Tory party, and it followed naturally that the Whig or Liberal party, being in antagonism to the party which had long kept the country under arms, should charge itself with the duty of expressing a just hatred of all wars which are needless or unjust. If speakers, in the performance of this duty, often used extravagant or fanatical language, they did not perhaps mean to inculcate much doctrine, but rather to display the vehemence of their hostility to the opposite faction. The applause which greeted these denunciations had the same meaning. On the other hand the Tories declared that they did not yield to their adversaries in hatred of all needless wars; and thus for near forty years, there was a chorus and an anti-chorus engaged in a continual chant, and denouncing wars in the abstract at times when no war seemed impending. To men skimming the surface of English politics it was made to appear that the people had a rooted love of peace.

These signs of a peaceful determination had increased in abundance after the great constitutional change which obliged the ruling classes to share their power with the people at large, and thence it was inferred that the desire of England to remain at peace was not the mere whim of any Administration or of any political party, but was based upon the solemn determination of the whole people; and it has been seen that the Emperor Nicholas had deliberately founded his policy upon this belief. A deeper knowledge might have taught him that a fiery, generous people is more quick to plunge into war, than a cold, worldly, politic oligarchy; and that, even if the policy of England were as much under the control of the masses of the people as he believed it to be, there would be all the more likelihood of her being prone to take up arms; because in States which are much under the governance of the democratic principle, a proposal to make war against the foreigner is often resorted to by one of the contending factions as a stratagem for baffling the others. But these truths lay below; and what appeared upon the surface of English politics was a sincere devotion to the cause of peace. Over and over again it was laid down, with the seeming concurrence of unanimous thousands, that war, if it were not for mere defence, was not only foolish, but was also in a high degree wicked.

But the English can hardly ever be governed by a dogma, for although they are by nature wise in action, yet, being vehement and careless in their way of applauding loud words, they encourage their orators, and those also who address them in writing, to be strenuous rather than wise; and the result is, that these teachers, trying always to be more and more forcible, grow blind to logical dangers, and leap with headlong joy into the wit which reasoners call the Absurdum. Then, and not without joyous laughter, reaction begins.

All England had been brought to the opinion that it was a wickedness to incur war without necessity or justice; but when the leading spirits of the Peace Party had the happiness of beholding this wholesome result, they were far from stopping short. They went on to make light of the very principles by which peace is best maintained, and although they were conscientious men, meaning to say and do what was right, yet, being unacquainted with the causes which bring about the fall of empires, they deliberately inculcated that habit of setting comfort against honour which historians call "corruption." They made it plain, as they imagined, that no war which was not engaged in for the actual defence of the country could ever be right; but even there they took no rest, for they went on and on, and still on, until their foremost thinker reached the conclusion that, in the event of an attack upon our shores, the invaders ought to be received with such an effusion of hospitality and brotherly love as could not fail to disarm them of their enmity, and convert the once dangerous Zouave into the valued friend of the family.* Then, with great merriment, the whole English people turned round, and although they might still be willing to go to the brink of other precipices, they refused to go further towards that one. The doctrine had struck no root. It was ill suited to the race to whom it was addressed. The male cheered it, and forgot it until there came a time for testing it, and then discarded it; and the woman, from the very first, with her true and simple instinct, was quick to understand its value. She would subscribe, if her husband required it, to have the doctrine taught to charity children, but she would not suffer it to be taught to her own boy. So it proved barren. In truth, the English knew that they were a great and a free people, because their fathers, and their fathers' fathers, and all the great ancestry of whom they come, had been men of warlike quality; and deeming it time to gainsay the teaching of the Peace Party, but not being skilled in dialectics and the use of words, they unconsciously

---

* I have no copy of this curious pamphlet before me, but it has been quoted (I believe by Lord Palmerston) in the House of Commons, and therefore the passage alluded to in the text might no doubt be found in Hansard. The writer, I remember, went further than is above stated. He argued that the French people would be so ashamed by the kindness shown to their troops that they would never rest until they had paid us a large pecuniary indemnity for any losses or inconvenience which the invasion may have caused.

CHAP. XXIV.
State of feeling in the spring of 1853.

came to think that it would be well to express a practical opinion of the doctrine by taking the first honest and fair opportunity of engaging in war. Still, the conscience of the nation was sound, and men were as well convinced as ever of the wickedness of a war wrongly or wantonly incurred. They were in this mind: they would not go to war without believing that they had a good and a just cause, but it was certain that tidings importing the necessity of going to war for duty's sake would be received with a welcome in England.

Effect of the Czar's aggression upon the public mind.

Therefore, when the people gradually came to hear of the fierce oppression attempted by Prince Mentschikoff, and the wise, firm, moderate resistance of the Turks, they believed that there might be coming in sight once more that very thing for which they longed in their hearts — namely, a just cause of war. And when at length the seemingly unequal conflict began, the bravery of the Turks on the Danube, and the skill of their General, quickly roused that sympathy which England hardly ever refuses to a valiant combatant who is weaker than his foe; but when they came to know of the catastrophe of Sinope, and to hear of it as a slaughter treacherously and stealthily committed upon their old ally by an enemy who had engaged to observe neutrality in the Euxine,* they were inflamed with a desire to

* The erroneousness of this impression has been already shown. See *ante*.

execute justice, and nothing was now wanting to fill the measure of their righteous anger except a disclosure of the Czar's cold scheme for the spoliation of the "sick man's" house.

But after all, and especially in questions of foreign policy, the bulk of a nation must lean for guidance upon public men; and unless it appear that there were Statesmen deserving the ear of the country who faithfully tried to make a stand against error and failed for want of public support, it is unfair to charge the fault upon the people. Still in foreign affairs the nation looks for guidance to public men.

There were two statesmen high in office, and high in the confidence of the nation, who, more than most other men, were known to be attached to the cause of peace. To them every man looked who desired that his country should not be drawn into war without stringent need.

The impression produced upon the Court of St Petersburg by the heedless language of our Prime Minister has been already described; but the effect which he wrought upon the public mind of England by remaining at the head of the Government is still to be shown. Lord Aberdeen's hatred of war was so honestly and piously entertained, and was, at the same time, so excessive and self-defeating, that in one point of view it had the character of a virtue, and in another it was more like disease. His feelings, no less than his opinions, turned him against Lord Aberdeen.

all war: but against a war with Russia he was biassed by the impressions of his early life; by the relation of mutual esteem which had long existed between the Emperor Nicholas and himself; and perhaps by a dim foresight of the perils which might be brought upon Europe by a forcible breaking-up of the ties established by the Congress of Vienna and riveted by the Peace of Paris. In an early stage of the dispute, he resolved that he would not remain at the head of the Government unless he could maintain peace; and he anxiously sought to choose a moment for making his stand against the further progress towards war. Far from wishing to prolong his hold of power, he was always labouring to make out when, and on what ground, he could lay down the burthen which oppressed him. Every day he passed his sure hour and a half in the Foreign Office, and came away more and more anxious perhaps, but without growing more clear-sighted. If he could ever have found the point where the road to peace diverged from the road to war, he would instantly have declared for peace; and, failing to carry the Government with him, would have joyfully resigned office, and for his deliverance would have offered up thanksgiving to Heaven. But his intellect, though not without high quality in it, was deficient in clearness and force. In troubled times it did not yield him light enough to walk by, and it had not the propelling power which was needed for pushing him into opportune action. In politics, though not in matters of faith, he wanted the sacred impulse which his Kirk is accustomed to call "the word of quickening." Lord Clarendon's polished despatches so forced his approval that he could never lay his hand upon one of them and make it the subject of a ministerial crisis. Yet day by day, without knowing it, the Prime Minister was assenting to a course of policy destined to end in a rupture. Lord Clarendon's pithy phrase was less applicable to the country at large than to the Prime Minister. It was strictly true that Lord Aberdeen drifted. He steadfastly faced towards peace, and was always being carried towards war. He remained at the head of the Government; and, the papers being withheld from Parliament, the country was led to imagine that all which it was possible to do or suffer for the sake of peace would be done and suffered by a Cabinet of which Lord Aberdeen was the chief.

CHAP. XXIV.

But there was another member of the Cabinet who was supposed to hold war in deep abhorrence. Mr Gladstone was Chancellor of the Exchequer; and since he was by virtue of his office the appointed guardian of the public purse, those pure and lofty principles which made him cling to peace were reinforced by an official sense of the harm which war inflicts by its costliness. Now it happened that, if he was famous for the splendour of his eloquence, for his unaffected piety, and for his blameless life,

Mr Gladstone.

he was celebrated far and wide for a more than common liveliness of conscience. He had once imagined it to be his duty to quit a Government, and to burst through strong ties of friendship and gratitude, by reason of a thin shade of difference on the subject of white or brown sugar. It was believed that, if he were to commit even a little sin, or to imagine an evil thought, he would instantly arraign himself before the dread tribunal which awaited him in his own bosom; and that, his intellect being subtle and microscopic, and delighting in casuistry and exaggeration, he would be likely to give his soul a very harsh trial, and treat himself as a great criminal for faults too minute to be visible to the naked eyes of laymen. His friends lived in dread of his virtues as tending to make him whimsical and unstable; and the practical politicians, conceiving that he was not to be depended upon for party purposes, and was bent upon none but lofty objects, used to look upon him as dangerous — used to call him behind his back a good man — a good man in the worst sense of the term. In 1853 it seemed only too probable that he might quit office upon an infinitely slight suspicion of the warlike tendency of the Government: but what appeared certain was, that if, upon the vital question of peace or war, the Government should depart by even a hair's-breadth from the right path, the Chancellor of the Exchequer would instantly refuse to be a partaker of their fault. He, and he before all other men, stood charged to give the alarm of danger; and there seemed to be no particle of ground for fearing that, like the Prime Minister, he would drift. The known watchfulness and alacrity of his conscience, and his power of detecting small germs of evil, led the world to think it impossible that he could be moving for months together in a wrong course without knowing it.

Now, from the beginning of the negotiations until the final rupture, Lord Aberdeen continued to be the Prime Minister, and Mr Gladstone the Chancellor of the Exchequer. The result was that, during the session of 1853, and the autumn which followed it, the presence of these two Ministers in the Cabinet was regarded as a guarantee of the peaceful tendency of the Government; and when, after the catastrophe of Sinope, it became hardly possible to doubt that war was at hand, the continuing responsibility of these good men seemed to dispense the most anxious lovers of peace from the duty of further questioning; for if Lord Aberdeen continued to head the Ministry which was leading the country into war, people thought he must have attained a bitter certainty that war was needed: and, on the other hand, it was clear that Mr Gladstone, remaining in office, and taking it upon his conscience to prepare funds for the bloody strife, was giving to the public a sure guarantee that the enterprise in which he helped to engage the country was blame-

CHAP.
XXIV.
less at the very least, and even perhaps pure and holy. It was thus that the conscience of the people got quieted. It was a hard task to have to argue that peace could be honestly and wisely maintained when Lord Aberdeen was levying war. None but a bold man could say that the war was needless or wicked, whilst Mr Gladstone was feeding it with his own hand.

It was thus that, by the course which Lord Aberdeen and Mr Gladstone had been taking, the efforts of those who loved peace were paralysed. No doubt a cold retrospect, carried on with the light of the past, may enable a political critic to fix upon more than one occasion when, holding the opinions which they did, these two Ministers might have resolved to make a stand for peace; and it is believed that, long before his death, Lord Aberdeen saw this and grieved: but if any man will honestly recall the state of his own feelings and opinions in the year 1853, he will find perhaps that he himself at the time was carried down by the flood of events; and when ho has submitted to this self-discipline, he will be the better able to understand that others, though honest and able, might easily lose their footing. At all events, the errors of Lord Aberdeen and Mr Gladstone, if errors they were, were only errors of judgment. The scrupulous purity of their motives has never been brought into question.

But if these were the causes which inclined the

bulk of the English people to desire or to assent to the war, they hardly yield reasons sufficing to show why the lesser number of men, who honestly thought that peace ought to be maintained, should suffer themselves to be overpowered without making stand enough to prove that they clung to their old faith, and that England, however warlike, was, at all events, not of one mind. The hottest defenders of the war-policy could hardly refuse to acknowledge that there was much semblance of reason on the side of their adversaries. No one could say that the interest which England had in the perfect independence of the Ottoman Empire was so obvious and so deep as to exclude all questioning; and even if a man were driven from that first ground, still, without being guilty of paradox, he might fairly dispute, and say that the independence of the Sultan was not really brought into peril by a form of words which, during some weeks, had received the approval of every one of the five great Powers.

But if these views were only plausible, there was another which was sound. It could be fairly maintained that the intrusion of Russia into two provinces lying far away on the south-eastern frontiers of Austria was no cause why England alone, nor why England and France together, should undertake to stand forward and perform, at their own charge and cost, a duty which attached upon Austria in the first place, and next upon Europe at large.

CHAP. XXIV.
Nor for want of oratorical power.

Of course, the actual and immediate success of any such struggle for the maintenance of peace was grievously embarrassed, in the way already shown, by the course which had been taken by Lord Aberdeen and Mr. Gladstone; but it is not the custom of the English to be utterly disheartened by political losses; and it happened that outside the Government Offices the cause of peace was headed by two men who had been powerful in their time, and who retained the qualities of mind and body by which, in former years, they had gained a great sway.

Mr Cobden and Mr Bright.

Mr Cobden and Mr Bright were members of the House of Commons. Both had the gift of a manly strenuous eloquence; and their diction, being founded upon English lore rather than upon shreds of weak Latin, went straight to the mind of their hearers. Of these men the one could persuade, the other could attack; and, indeed, Mr. Bright's oratory was singularly well qualified for preventing an erroneous acquiescence in the policy of the day; for, besides that he was honest and fearless — besides that, with a ringing voice, he had all the clearness and force which resulted from his great natural gifts, as well as from his one-sided method of thinking — he had the advantage of being generally able to speak in a state of sincere anger. In former years, whilst their minds were disciplined by the almost mathematic exactness of the reasonings on which they relied, and when they were acting in concert with the shrewd traders of the north who had a very plain object in view, these two orators had shown with what a strength, with what a masterly skill, with what patience, with what a high courage, they could carry a great scientific truth through the storms of politics. They had shown that they could arouse and govern the assenting thousands who listened to them with delight — that they could bend the House of Commons — that they could press their creed upon a Prime Minister, and put upon his mind so hard a stress that, after a while, he felt it to be a torture and a violence to his reason to have to make stand against them. Nay, more! each of these two gifted men had proved that he could go bravely into the midst of angry opponents — could show them their fallacies one by one — destroy their favourite theories before their very faces, and triumphantly argue them down. Now these two men were honestly devoted to the cause of peace. They honestly believed that the impending war with Russia was a needless war. There was no stain upon their names. How came it that they sank, and were able to make no good stand for the cause they loved so well?

The answer is simple.

Upon the question of peace or war (the very question upon which more than any other a man might well desire to make his counsels tell) these two gifted men had forfeited their hold upon the ear of the country. They had forfeited it by their former

CHAP. XXIV.

Reasons why they were able to make no stand.

CHAP.
XXIV.
want of moderation. It was not by any intemperate words upon the question of this war with Russia that they had shut themselves out from the counsels of the nation; but in former years they had adopted and put forward, in their strenuous way, some of the more extravagant doctrines of the Peace Party. In times when no war was in question, they had run down the practice of war in terms so broad and indiscriminate that they were understood to commit themselves to a disapproval of all wars not strictly defensive, and to decline to treat as defensive those wars which, although not waged against an actual invader of the Queen's dominions, might still be undertaken by England in the performance of an European duty, or for the purpose of checking the undue ascendancy of another Power. Of course the knowledge that they held doctrines of this wide sort disqualified them from arguing with any effect against the war then impending. A man cannot have weight as an opponent of any particular war if he is one who is known to be against almost all war. It is vain for him to offer to be moderate for the nonce, and to propose to argue the question in a way which his hearers will recognise. In vain he declares that for the sake of argument he will lay aside his own broad principles and mimic the reasoning of his hearers. Practical men know that his mind is under the sway of an antecedent determination which dispenses him from the more narrow but more important

inquiry in which they are engaged. They will not give ear to one who is striving to lay down the conclusions which ought, as he says, to follow from other men's principles. He who altogether abjures the juice of the grape cannot usefully criticise the vintage of any particular year; and a man who is the steady adversary of wars in general, upon broad and paramount grounds, will never be regarded as a sound judge of the question whether any particular war is wicked or righteous, nor whether it is foolish or wise.

It must be added that there was another cause which tended to disqualify Mr Bright from taking an effective part in the maintenance of peace. For one who would undertake a task of that kind at a time when warlike ardour is prevailing in the country, it is above all things necessary that he should be a statesman so truly attached to what men mean when they talk of their country, and so jealous of its honour, that no man could ascribe his efforts in the cause of peace to motives which a warlike and high-spirited people would repudiate. Mr Bright sincerely desired the welfare of the traders and workmen in the United Kingdom; and if he desired the welfare of the other classes of the people with less intensity, it may fairly be believed that to all he wished to see justice done: so, if this worthy disposition of mind were equivalent to what a man calls his "love of his country," no one could fairly say that Mr Bright was without the passion. But, in another, and certainly the old and the usual sense, a man's love "of his country" is understood to represent something more than common benevolence towards the persons living within it. For if he be the citizen of an ancient State blessed with freedom, renowned in arms, and holding wide sway in the world, his love of his country means something of attachment to the institutions which have made her what she is—means something of pride in the long suffering, and the battle, and the strife which have shed glory upon his countrymen in his own time, and upon their fathers in the time before him. It means that he feels his country's honour to be a main term and element of his own content. It means that he is bent upon the upholding of her dominion, and is so tempered as to become the sudden enemy of any man who, even though he be not an invader, still attempts to hack at her power. Now in this the heathen, but accustomed sense of the phrase, Mr Bright would be the last to say that he was a lover of his country. He would rather, perhaps, acknowledge that, taking "his country" in that sense, he hated it. Yet at a time when the spirit of the nation was up, no man could usefully strive to moderate or guide it unless his patriotism were believed to be exactly of that heathen sort which Mr Bright disapproved. Thus, by the nature of his patriotism no less than by the immoderate width of his views on the lawfulness of wars, this powerful orator was so disabled as to be hindered from applying his strength towards the maintenance of peace.

The country was impassioned, but it was not so mad as to be deaf to precious counsels; and a statesman who had shown by his past life that he loved his country in the ancient way, and that he knew how to contemplate the eventuality of war with a calm and equal mind, might have won attention for views which questioned the necessity of the war then threatened; and if, in good time, he had brought to bear upon his opinions a sufficing power and knowledge, he might have altered the policy of his country.* But outside the Cabinet the real tenor of the negotiations of 1853 was still unknown; and Lord Aberdeen and Mr Gladstone consenting to remain members of a war-going Government, and Mr Cobden and Mr Bright being disqualified for useful debate by the nature of their opinions, no stand could be made.

* This was in print before that curious and interesting confirmation of my statement — my statement of the relations between the Peace Party and their country — which Mr Cobden has since given to the world. Mr Cobden has said that at the time of the war neither he nor Mr Bright could win any attention to their views; and he added that he (Mr Cobden) will never again try to withstand a warlike ardour once kindled, because, when a people are inflamed in that way, they are no better than "mad dogs." — *Speech in the autumn of 1862.* He sees no defect in the principles of a Peace Party which is to suspend its operations in times of warlike excitement.

CHAP. XXIV.

By these steps, then, the English people passed from a seeming approval of the doctrines of the Peace Party to a state of warlike ardour; and it was plain that, if the Queen should send down to the Houses of Parliament a message importing war, the Royal appeal would be joyfully answered by an almost unanimous people.

CHAPTER XXV.

WHEN the English Parliament assembled on the 31st of January, there was still going on in Europe a semblance of negotiation; but amongst men accustomed to the aspect of public affairs, there was hardly more than one who failed to see that France and England had gone too far to be able to recede, and that, by the very weight of their power and its inherent duties, they were now at last drawn into war. This condition of things was fairly enough disclosed by the Queen's Speech, and Parliament was asked to provide for an increase of the military and naval forces, with a view to give weight to the negotiations still pending. But the English Government was not suffered to forget its bond with the French Emperor; and the Prime Minister, whilst still indulging a hope of peace, consented to record and continue the error which had brought him to the verge of war. It seems that for good reasons it was of some moment to the French Emperor to be signally named in the Queen's Speech; and Lord Aberdeen again submitted to a form of words which carefully distinguished the posture of France and England from that of the four Powers. The Queen was advised to say: "I have continued to act in cordial "co-operation with the Emperor of the French; and "my endeavours in conjunction with my Allies to "preserve and to restore peace between the con- "tending parties, although hitherto unsuccessful, have "been unremitting."

<small>The policy which it indicated.</small>

<small>The separate understanding with France not justified by any difference of opinion between England and the German Powers.</small>

<small>Unswerving resolve of Austria (and Prussia supports her) to rid the Principalities of Russian troops.</small>

Like the similar paragraph which had marked the Royal Speech at the close of the preceding session, this phrase, strange as it was, gave a true though somewhat dim glimpse of the policy which was leading England astray. In principle she was marching along with all the rest of the four Powers, and yet all the while she was engaged with the French Emperor in a separate course of action. If the aims of Austria and Prussia had been seriously at variance with those of the Western Powers, this difference might have been a good reason for separate action on the part of France and England. But the contrary was true. So deep was the interest of Austria in the cause, and so closely were her views approved by Prussia, that although for several months France and England had been pressing forward in a way which seemed to endanger the coherence of the quadruple union, still even this dangerous course had hitherto failed to destroy the unanimity of the four Powers. If the French Emperor sought to use his alliance with England as a means of strengthening his hold over France, and if England was beginning to love the thought of war for war's sake,

Austria, from motives of a higher and more cogent sort (for she saw her interests vitally touched, and her safety threatened), was eager and determined to take such steps as might be needed for delivering the Principalities. Prussia agreed with her. It was nothing but the impatience and forwardness of France and England which relieved Austria from the necessity of taking the lead; for the wrong which had to be redressed was one from which she of all the great Powers was the most a sufferer; and she had the concurrence of Prussia not only in regard to the existing state of things, but even as to the ulterior objects of the war which her resolve might bring upon Germany.

The proofs of all this abound. By the repeated words of responsible statesmen, by despatches, by collective notes, by protocols, by solemn treaty of offensive and defensive alliance against Russia, by peremptory summons addressed to the Czar, and, finally (so far as concerns Austria), by the application of force, the German Powers disclosed and executed their policy; and the policy which they so disclosed and executed was the same policy as had been avowed by the Western Powers. It has been seen that in that early period of the troubles, when the Czar was but beginning to cross the Pruth, Austria took upon herself to endeavour to form a league for forcing the Czar to relinquish the Principalities; and from that hour down to the time when Nicholas gave way and re-entered his own dominions, her efforts to bring about this end were unceasing and restless.

Of the spirit in which Austria was acting through all the early stages of the negotiations, many a proof has been already given. With time her impatience of the Czar's intrusion upon her southern frontier increased and increased. It is true that she did not desire war: she anxiously wished to avoid it. She wished, if it were possible, to achieve the end without war, but to achieve it she was resolved; and if a vestige of the mediating character which had belonged to her in the summer of 1853, or her legitimate anxiety to spare the Czar's personal feelings, was a motive which tended to soften her language, it did not deflect her policy. Count Buol declared that although, in treating with Russia, "more management of terms"* was required from Austria than from the Western Powers, the objects sought by all the four Powers were the same, and that they ought to be compassed by "a general con-"cordance in the way of putting them forward."** But even the notion of using a gentler form of expression than the one employed by the Western Powers was quickly abandoned, and Austria found no difficulty in adopting the exact words of the collective Note framed by Lord Clarendon in concert with the French Government. So anxious was Austria to remain on the same ground with the rest of the

---

* "Eastern Papers," part vii. p. 231.
** Ibid. p. 278.

four Powers, that she came into every term of the firm and wise scheme of action laid down by Lord Clarendon on the 16th of November,* and bitterly offended the Czar by agreeing, at Lord Clarendon's instance, that the Porte should not be even asked to accept any condition which it had already rejected, and by affirming the determination of the four Powers to intervene in any settlement of the dispute between Russia and Turkey.

Prussia also gave her unreserved adhesion to the plan of action laid down by Lord Clarendon and to the measures resulting from it.** By the Protocol of the 5th of December 1853*** both Austria and Prussia joined with the Western Powers in declaring that the existence of Turkey in the limits assigned to it by existing treaties was one of the necessary conditions of the European equilibrium.

By the Protocol of the 13th of January the four Powers recorded their approval of the terms agreed to by the Turkish Government, and resolved to submit them to the Court of St Petersburg. At the very time when the English Government were framing the Speech from the Throne which ostentatiously separated France and England from the rest of the four Powers, the two great Courts of Germany were sending back Count Orloff and Baron Budberg to St Petersburg, not only with a refusal

---

* "Eastern Papers," part vii. pp. 238, 258.
** Ibid. part ii. p. 263.
*** Ibid. p. 296.

on their part to give any engagement to stand neutral, but with a plain avowal that they intended to remain faithful to the principles which the four Powers had adopted in concert. Prussia told Baron Budberg that she should have to devise means without Russia for maintaining the equilibrium of Europe. In significant words the Emperor Francis Joseph told Count Orloff that he should have to be guided by the interests and the dignity of his Empire.

It is said that, by the tidings which forced him to know that he was alienated from the Austrian Emperor, the Czar was wounded deep. He had conceived a strong affection for Francis Joseph, and wherever he went he carried with him a small statuette which recalled to his mind the features of the youthful Kaiser. It would seem that his affection was of the kind which a loving and yet stern father bears his son, for it was joined with a sense of right to exact a great deference to his will. Nicholas had been strangely slow to believe that Francis Joseph could harbour the thought of opposing him in arms; and when at last the truth was forced upon him, he desired that the marble should be taken from his sight. But he did not, they say, speak in anger. When he had spoken he covered his face with his hands and was wrung with grief.

What we are showing just now is the complete union of opinion which was existing between England and the two great Courts of Germany on the 31st of

January 1854, and in order to this we have already referred to a variety of diplomatic transactions coming down to the time in question; but the policy of the Courts of Vienna and Berlin at the close of the month of January is to be inferred, of course, from the transactions which followed this date, as well as from those which preceded it; and therefore it will be convenient to go forward a little in advance of the general progress of the narrative, in order to bring under one view the grounds which support our proposition.

Day by day the joint pressure of the four Powers became more cogent. By the Protocol of the 2d of February the four Powers unanimously rejected the counter-propositions made by Russia. On the 14th of March both Austria and Prussia addressed circulars to the Courts of the German Confederation, in which they pointed out that the interests in question were essentially German interests, and that the active co-operation of Germany might be needed. On the 18th of March the King of Prussia asked his Chamber for an extraordinary credit of thirty million of thalers; and he at the same time declared that he would not swerve from the principles established by the Vienna Conference, and would faithfully protect every member of the Confederation who, at an earlier moment than Prussia, might be called on to draw the sword for the defence of German interests.

Nor were these bare words. Austria, it has been already said, was so placed that, whatever dangers

Proofs drawn from transactions subsequent to the Queen's Speech.

she might draw upon her other frontiers, she could act with irresistible pressure upon the invader of the Principalities. On the 6th and 22d of February she reinforced her army on the frontier of Wallachia by 50,000 men, and thus placed the Russian army of occupation completely at her mercy. On the day when she sent that last reinforcement into the Banat, she had grown so impatient of the further continuance of the Russians in the Principalities that she actually pressed France and England to summon Russia to quit the Principalities under pain of a declaration of war, and undertook to support their summons.* Prussia was approving; and on the 25th Baron Manteuffel wrote to Count Arnim at Vienna "on the subject of the more decided policy "which it was supposed the Austrian Government "was about to adopt in the affairs of the East, and "expressed the satisfaction of the Prussian Govern- "ment at the interests of Germany on the Danube "being likely to be so warmly espoused."** On the 2d of March the French Emperor had so little doubt of the concurrence of Austria and Germany, that he announced it in his Speech from the Throne. "Ger- "many," said he, "has recovered her independence, "and has looked freely to see whither her true inter- "ests led her. Austria especially, who cannot see "with indifference the events going on, will join our "alliance, and will thus come to confirm the morality

* "Eastern Papers," part vii. p. 53.
** Ibid. p. 64.

"and justice of the war which we undertake. We go to Constantinople with Germany."

On the 20th of March the four Powers were so well agreed that, when Greece sought to make a diversion in favour of Russia, the representatives of Austria, Prussia, France, and England, all joined in a collective Note, which called upon the Greek Government, in terms approaching menace, to give way to the demands of the Porte. On the very day which followed the English declaration of war, the Emperor of Austria appointed the Archduke Albert to the command of the forces on the frontier of Wallachia, and at the same time the "Third Army" was put upon the war footing. A little later[*] the Emperor of Austria ordered a new levy of 95,000 men for the defence of his frontiers. Later still, but within one day[**] of the time when France and England were making their alliance, Austria and Prussia joined with France and England in a Protocol, which not only recorded the fact that the hostile step then just taken by France and England was "supported by Austria and Prussia as being founded "in right," but went on to declare that "at that "solemn moment the Governments of the four Powers "remained united in their object of maintaining the "integrity of the Ottoman Empire, of which the fact "of the evacuation of the Danubian Principalities is "and will remain one of the essential conditions;"

[*] May 15.
[**] April 9, 1854.

"and that the territorial integrity of the Ottoman "Empire is and remains the *sine quâ non* condition "of every transaction having for its object the re-"establishment of peace between the belligerent "Powers." Finally, the Protocol stipulated that none of the "four Powers should enter into any definitive "arrangement with the Imperial Court of Russia "which should be at variance with the principles "declared by the Protocol without first deliberating "thereon in common."*

On the 20th of April Austria and Prussia contracted with each other an offensive and defensive alliance, by which they guaranteed to each other all their respective possessions, so that an attack upon the territory of one should be regarded by the other as an act of hostility against his own territory, and engaged to hold a part of their forces in perfect readiness for war. By the Second Article they declared that they stood "engaged to defend the "rights and interests of Germany against all and "every injury, and to consider themselves bound "accordingly for the mutual repulse of every attack "on any part whatsoever of their territories; likewise, "also, in the case where one of the two may find "himself, in understanding with the others, obliged "to advance actively for the defence of German in-"terests."**

By the Additional Article they declared "that

---

* "Eastern Papers," part viii. p. 2.
** Ibid. part ix. p. 3.

"the indefinite continuance of the occupation of the
"territories on the Lower Danube, under the sover-
"eignty of the Ottoman Porte, by imperial Russian
"troops, would endanger the political, moral, and
"material interests of the whole German Confederation
"as also of their own States, and the more so as
"Russia extends her warlike operations on Turkish
"territory;" and then went on to stipulate "that
"the Austrian Government should address a com-
"munication to the Russian Court, with the object
"of obtaining from the Emperor of Russia the
"necessary orders for putting an immediate stop
"to the further advance of his armies upon the
"Turkish territory, as also to request of His Imperial
"Majesty sufficient guarantees for the prompt eva-
"cuation of the Danubian Principalities, and that
"the Prussian Government should again, in the most
"energetic manner, support these communications."
Finally, the high contracting parties agreed that,
"if, contrary to expectation, the answer of the Russian
"Court should not be of a nature to give them entire
"satisfaction, the measures to be taken by one of the
"contracting parties, according to the terms of Ar-
"ticle II. signed on that day, would be on the under-
"standing that every hostile attack on the territory
"of one of the contracting parties should be repelled
"with all the military forces at the disposal of the
"other."*

* "Eastern Papers," part ii.

Of the intent and the meaning of this treaty, and the use which Austria and Prussia were about to make of it, no doubt could exist. Failing the peremptory summons which was to be addressed to Russia, the forces of Austria alone were to execute the easy task of expelling the troops of the Czar from the Principalities; and in order to withstand the vengeance which this step might provoke, Austria and Prussia together stood leagued.

By the Protocol of the 23d of May, the four Powers declared that both the Anglo-French treaty and the Austro-Prussian treaty bound the parties, in the relative situations to which they applied, to secure the same common object — namely, the evacuation of the Principalities and the integrity of the Ottoman Empire.*

Now the mind and the solemn determination of Austria and Prussia being such as are shown by the Protocol of the 9th and the treaty of the 20th April, where was there such a difference of opinion — where was there even such a shadow of a difference — as to justify the Western States in pushing forward and separating themselves from the rest of the four Powers? The avowed principles and objects of the four Powers were exactly the same. If they had acted together, the very weight of their power would have given them an almost judicial authority, and would have enabled them to enforce the cause of

---

* "Eastern Papers," part ix. p. 1.

right without wounding the pride of the disturber, and without inflicting war upon Europe.

Was Austria backward? Was she so little prone to action that it was necessary for the Western Powers to move to the front and fight her battles for her? The reverse is the truth. The Western Powers, indeed, were more impatient than Germany was to go through the forms which were necessary for bringing themselves legally into a state of war, but for action of a serious kind they were not yet ready. Whilst they were only preparing, Austria was applying force. On the 3d of June, with the full support of Prussia, she summoned the Emperor Nicholas to evacuate the Principalities. Her summons was the summons of a Power having an army on the edge of the province into which the Russian forces had been rashly extended. Such a summons was a mandate. The Czar could not disobey it. He could not stand in Wallachia when he was called upon to quit the province by a Power which had assembled its forces upon his flank and rear. He sought, indeed, to make terms, but the German Powers were peremptory. On the 14th Austria entered into a convention with the Porte, which not only legalized her determination to drive the Russian forces from the Principalities, and to occupy them with her own troops, but which formally joined Austria in an alliance with the Porte against Russia; for, by the 1st Article of the convention, the Emperor of Austria "engages to exhaust all the means

CHAP. XXV.

"of negotiation, and all other means, to obtain the "evacuation of the Danubian Principalities by the "foreign army which occupies them, and even to "employ, in case they are required, the number of "troops necessary to attain this end."* And since Russia could not invade European Turkey by land without marching through the Principalities, this undertaking by Austria involved an engagement to free the Sultan's land frontiers in Europe from Russian invasion. Exactly at the same time** Austria and Prussia addressed notes to the Powers represented at the Conference of Bamberg, in which the liberation of the commerce and navigation of the Danube was held out to Germany as the object to be obtained.

The time when the interests of Austria and Prussia began to divide them from the Western Powers.

Austria was upon the brink of war with Russia, was preparing to take forcible possession of the Principalities, and had despatched an officer to the English headquarters with a view to concert a joint scheme of military operations, when the Czar at length gave way, and abandoned the whole of the territory which, under the nauseous description of a "material guarantee," had become the subject of war. Other causes, as will be seen, were conducing to this result; but none were so cogent as the forcible pressure which Austria had exerted, by first assembling forces in the Banat and then summoning the Czar to withdraw from the invaded provinces.

* "Eastern Papers," part xii.
** 14th and 16th of June.

Of course, when the object which called forth the German Powers was attained, and when it transpired (as it did at the same time) that the Western Powers were resolved to abandon the common field of action, and to undertake the invasion by sea of a distant Russian province inaccessible to Austria and Prussia, then at last, and then for the first time, the German Powers found that their interests were parting them from the great maritime States of the West; for in one and the same week they were relieved from the grievance which was their motive for action, and deprived of all hope of support from the Western Powers; but it is certain that from the moment when the Czar first seized the Principalities to that in which he recrossed the Pruth, the determination of Austria to put an end to the intrusion was never languid, and was always increasing in force. It is certain, also, that up to the time when the relinquishment of the Principalities began, there was no defection on the part of Prussia;* and that the minor States of Germany, fully alive to the importance of a struggle which promised to free the great outlet of the

side note: CHAP. XXV. From first to last Austria and Prussia never swerved from their resolve to secure the Czar's relinquishment of the Principalities.

---

* Prussia began to hang back, it seems, on about the 21st of July. "Eastern Papers," part xi. p. 1; and this was exactly the time when her interests counselled her to do so; for by that day she knew that the deliverance of the Principalities was secured and in process of execution, and had also no doubt learned of the determination of the Western Powers to move their forces to the Crimea, thereby uncovering Germany. Austria, with similar motives for separation, was less inclined to part from the Western Powers. See her Note of the 8th August 1854, and the various diplomatic transactions in which she took part down to the close of the war.

CHAP. XXV.

Danube from Russian dominion, were resolved to support Austria and Prussia with the troops of the Confederation.* As soon as the Principalities were relinquished by the Czar they were occupied by Austrian troops, in pursuance of the convention with the Porte; and thus the outrage, which during twelve months had disturbed the tranquillity of Europe, was then at last finally repressed.

* 20th July 1854. The relinquishment of the Principalities virtually began on the 16th of June — the day when the siege of Silistria was raised — and before the end of July the Russian forces had quitted the capital of Wallachia. On the 2d of August they repassed the Pruth.

CHAPTER XXVI.

For the sake of bringing under one view the course of action followed by the German Powers, down to the moment when their object was achieved by the deliverance of the Principalities, it has been necessary, as we have said, to go forward in advance of the period reached by the main thread of the narrative. The subject thus quitted for a moment and now resumed is the policy which was disclosed by the English Government upon the opening of Parliament.

Distinct from the martial ardour already kindled in England, there had sprung up amongst the people an almost romantic craving for warlike adventure, and this feeling was not slow to reach the Cabinet. Now, without severance from the German Powers, there could plainly be little prospect of adventure; for, besides that the German monarchs desired to free the Principalities with as little resort to hostilities as might be compatible with the attainment of the end, it was almost certain that the policy of keeping up the perfect union and co-operation of the four Powers would prevent war by its overwhelming

CHAP. XXVI.

Spirit of warlike adventure in England.

CHAP. XXVI.

The bearing of this spirit upon the policy of the Government.

force. Like the power of the law, it would operate by coercion, and not by clangour of arms. This was a merit; but it was a merit fatal to its reception in England. The popularity of such a policy was nearly upon the same modest level as the popularity of virtue. All whose volitions were governed by the imagined rapture of freeing Poland, or destroying Cronstadt and lording it with our flag in the Baltic — or taking the command of the Euxine, and sinking the Russian fleet under the guns of Sebastopol; all who meant to raise Circassia, and cut off the Muscovite from the glowing South by holding the Dariel Pass, and those also who dwelt in fancy upon deeds to be done on the shores of the Caspian; — all these, and many more, saw plainly enough that separation from the German Powers and alliance with the new Bonaparte was the only road to adventure. Lord Aberdeen was not one of these, but it was his fate to act as though he were. He was not without a glimmering perception that the firmly maintained union of the four Powers meant peace:* but he saw the truth dimly; and there being a certain slowness in his high intellectual nature, he was not so touched by his belief as to be able to make it the guide of his action. He seems to have gone on imagining that, consistently with the maintenance of a perfect union of the four Powers, there might be a separate and

---

* 126 Hansard, p. 1650.

still more perfect union between two of them, and that this kind of alliance within alliance was a structure not fatal — nay, even perhaps conducive — to peace.

And, after all, England was not free: she was bound to the French Emperor. No treaty of alliance had been signed, but the understanding disclosed in the summer of the year before was still riveted upon the members of the English Government. They had been drawn into a weighty engagement in 1853, and now they had to perform it. In the midst of perfect concord between her and her three allies, England had to stand forward with one of them in advance of the rest, and thus ruin that security for the maintenance of peace which depended upon the united action of the four great Powers. As the price of his consenting to join reluctant France in an alliance with Turkey, the French Emperor was justly entitled to insist on the other terms of the bond, and not only to be signally coupled with England in a course of action which was to separate her from the great German States, but to have it blazoned out to the world beforehand that, distinctly from the concord of the four Powers, the Queen of England and he were acting together. The Royal Speech of January 1854 was as clear in this as the Speech of the previous August. Both disclosed a separate understanding with the French Emperor. In both, as any one could see who was used to State writings,

England was under engagements with the French Emperor.

CHAP.
XXVI.

the mark was set upon England with the same branding-iron.

Into this policy the bulk of the Cabinet drifted.

To a man looking back upon the past, it seems strange that a Cabinet of English statesmen could have been led to adopt this singular policy. It would seem that, with many of the Cabinet, the tendency of the measures which they were sanctioning was concealed from them by the gentleness of the incline on which they moved; and if there were some of them who had a clearer view of their motives, it must be inferred that they acted upon grounds not yet disclosed to the world. Of course, what the welfare of the State required was a Ministry which shared and honoured the public feeling, without being so carried down by it as to lose the statesman's power of understanding and controlling events. But this was not given. Of the bulk of the Cabinet, and possibly of all of them except one, Lord Clarendon's pithy phrase was the true one, — they drifted. Wishing to control events, they were controlled by them. They aimed to go in one direction; but, lapsing under pressure of forces external and misunderstood, they always went in the other.

The Minister who went his own way.

The statesman who went his own way was one whose share in the governance of events was not much known. He was supposed to be under a kind of ostracism. He had not been banished from England, nor even from the Cabinet; but, holding office under a Prime Minister whose views upon foreign policy were much opposed to his own, and relegated to duties connected with the peaceful administration of justice, it seemed to the eye of the common observer that for the time he was annulled; and the humorous stories which floated about Whitehall went to show that the deposed Lord of Foreign Affairs had consented to forget his former greatness and to accept his Home Office duties in a spirit of half-cynical, half-joyous disdain, but without the least discontent. And, in truth, he had no ground for ill-humour. In politics he was without vanity. What he cared for was power, and power he had. Indeed, circumstanced as he then was, he must have known that one of the main conditions of his strength was the general belief that he had none. The light of the past makes it easy to see that the expedient of trying to tether him down in the Home Office would alleviate his responsibility and increase his real power. To those who know anything of Lord Palmerston's intellectual power, of his boldness, his vast and concentrated energy, his instinct for understanding the collective mind of a body of men and of a whole nation, and, above all, his firm robust will; nay, even to those who only know of his daring achievements — achievements half peaceful, half warlike, half righteous, half violent in many lands, and on many a sea — the notion of causing him to be subordinated to Lord Aberdeen in Foreign Affairs seems hardly more sound than a scheme providing that the greater shall be contained in the less. Statesmen on the

CHAP.
XXVI.
Continent would easily understand this, for they had lived much under the weight of his strenuous nature; but at that time he had not been much called upon to apply his energies to the domestic affairs of England. Besides, he had been more seen in his own country than abroad, and for that very reason he was less known, because there was much upon the mere outside which tended to mask his real nature. His partly Celtic blood, and perhaps too, in early life, his boyish consciousness of power, had given him a certain elation of manner and bearing which kept him for a long time out of the good graces of the more fastidious part of the English world. The defect was toned down by age, for it lay upon the surface only, and in his inner nature there was nothing vulgar nor unduly pretending. Still, the defect made people slow — made them take forty years — to recognise the full measure of his intellectual strength. Moreover, the English had so imperfect a knowledge of the stress which he had long been putting upon foreign Governments, that the mere outward signs which he gave to his countrymen at home — his frank speech, his offhand manner, his ready banter, his kind, joyous, beaming eyes — were enough to prevent them from accustoming themselves to look upon him as a man of stern purpose. Upon the whole, notwithstanding his European fame, it was easy for him at this time to escape grave attention in England.

He was not a man who would come to a subject

with which he was dealing for the first time with any great store of preconceived opinions, but he wrote so strenuously — he always, they say, wrote standing — and was apt to be so much struck with the cogency of his own arguments, that by the mere process of framing despatches he wrought himself into strong convictions, or rather perhaps into strong resolves; and he clung to these with such a lasting tenacity that, if he had been a solemn, austere personage, the world would have accused him of pedantry. Like most gifted men who evolve their thoughts with a pen, he was very clear, very accurate. Of every subject which he handled gravely, he had a tight, iron grasp. Without being inflexible, his will, it has been already said, was powerful, and it swung with a great momentum in one direction until, for some good and sound reason, it turned and swung in another. He pursued one object at a time without being distracted by other game. All that was fanciful, or for any reason unpractical — all that was the least bit too high for him or the least bit too deep for him — all that lay, though only by a little, beyond the immediate future with which he was dealing — he utterly drove from out of his mind; and his energies, condensed for the time upon some object to which they could be applied with effect, were brought to bear upon it with all their full volume and power. So, during the whole period of his reign at the Foreign Office, Lord Palmerston's method had been to be very strenuous in the pursuit of the object which might be needing care at any given time, without suffering himself to be embarrassed by what men call a "comprehensive" view of our foreign policy; and although it was no doubt his concentrative habit of mind and his stirring temperament which brought him into this course of action, he was much supported in it by the people at home; for when no enterprise is on foot, the bulk of the English are prone to be careless of the friendship of foreign States, and are often much pleased when they are told that by reason of the activity of their Foreign Secretary they are without an ally in Europe.

Other statesmen had been accustomed to think that the principle which ought in general to determine the closeness of our relations with foreign States was "community of interests;" and that in proportion as this principle was departed from, under the varied impulses of philanthropy or other like motives, disturbance, isolation, and danger would follow; but Lord Palmerston had never suffered this maxim to interfere with any special object which he might chance to have in hand at the moment, nor even with his desire to spread abroad the blessings of constitutional government.

As long as Lord Grey was at the head of the Government, the energy of the Foreign Office was kept down; and even after the first five years of Lord Melbourne's Administration the disruption towards which it was tending had made so little way, that when in 1840 the Ottoman Empire was threatened with ruin by France and her Egyptian ally, Lord Palmerston, with a majority of only two or three in the House of Commons, but having a bold heart and a firm steady hand, had been able to gather up the elements of the great alliance of 1814, and to prevent a European war by the very might and power and swiftness with which he executed his policy; but at the end of eleven more years,[*] when his career at the Foreign Office was drawing to a close, his energy had cleared a space round him, and he seemed to be left standing alone.

His system by that time had fairly disclosed its true worth. Pursued with great vigour and skill, it had brought results corresponding with the numerous aims of its author, but corresponding also with his avowed disregard of a general guiding principle. Without breaking the general peace of Europe, it had produced a long series of diplomatic enterprises, pushed on in most instances to a successful issue; but, on the other hand, it had ended by making the Foreign Office an object of distrust, and in that way withdrawing England from her due place in the composition of the European system; for the good old safe clue of "community of interests" being visi-

---

[*] It is not forgotten that during a large portion of this last period Lord Aberdeen was at the Foreign Office, but he was of course much bound by what his predecessors had been doing before him; and, speaking roughly, it may be said that, from the spring of 1835 until the close of 1841, our foreign policy bore the impress of Lord Palmerston's mind. In the period between November 1830 and the autumn of 1834, it was much governed by the then Prime Minister, Lord Grey.

bly discarded, no Power, however closely bound to us by the nature of things, could venture to rely upon our friendship. States whose interests in great European questions were exactly the same as our own, States which had always looked to the welfare and strength of England as main conditions of their own safety, found no more favour with us than those who consumed much of their revenue in preparing implements for the slaughter of Englishmen and the sinking of English ships. They were therefore obliged to shape their policy upon the supposition that any slight matter in which the Foreign Office might chance to be interesting itself at the moment — nay, even a difference of opinion upon questions of internal government (and this, be it remembered, was an apple which could always be thrown) — would be enough to make England repulse them. From this cause, perhaps, more than from any other, there had sprung up in Germany that semblance of close friendship with the Court of St. Petersburg which had helped to allure the Czar into dangerous paths.

From the Emperor Nicholas, Lord Palmerston was cut off, not only by differences arising out of questions on which the policy of Russia and of England might naturally clash, but also because he was looked upon as the promoter of doctrines which the Court of St Petersburg was accustomed to treat as revolutionary. Even to Austria, although we were close bound to her by common interests, although there was no one national interest which tended to divide us from her, he had in this way become antagonistic. He had too much lustiness of mind, too much simplicity of purpose, to be capable of living on terms of close intelligence with the philosophical statesmen of Berlin. To the accustomed foreign policy of French statesmen — in other words, to the France that he had been used to encounter in the Foreign Office — he was adverse by very habit. He spurned the whole invention of the French Republic. But his favourite hatred of all was his hatred of the House of Bourbon.* In short, by the 1st of December 1851, though still at the Foreign Office, he had become isolated in Europe. But fortune smiles on bold men. The next night Prince Louis Bonaparte and his fellow-venturers destroyed the French Republic, superseded the Bourbons, and suppressed France. Plainly this Prince and Lord Palmerston were men who could act together — could act together until the Prince should advise himself to deceive the English Minister. Not longer: not an hour beyond the time when the momentous promise which was made, if I mistake not, before the events of December, should remain unbroken.

So when the Czar began to encroach upon the Sultan there was nothing that could so completely meet Lord Palmerston's every wish as an alliance

---

* This feeling probably drew its origin from the business of the "Spanish Marriages."

between the two Western Powers, which should toss France headlong into the English policy of upholding the Ottoman Empire; and the price of this was a price which, far from grudging, he would actually delight to pay; for desiring to have the Governments of France and England actively united together for an English object — desiring to prevent a revival of the French Republic — and, above all, to prevent a restoration of the House of Bourbon — he was only too glad to be able to strengthen the new Emperor's hold upon France by exalting his personal station, and giving him the support of a close, separate, and published alliance with the Queen of England. And in regard to the dislocation which such a new policy might work, he seems not to have set so high a value upon the existing framework of the European system as to believe that its destruction would be a portentous evil. If he thought it an evil at all, he thought it one which a strong man might repair. He yet lives, and now this very task is upon him. He meets it without suffering himself to be distracted by the remnant of any old illusion; he meets it, too, as becomes him, without shrinking or fear. A resolute people stand round him. Upon the issue of this, his last and mightiest labour, his fame, he well knows, will have to rest.

Lord Palmerston had been at the head of the Foreign Office during so many years of his life, and he had brought to bear upon its duties an activity so restless, and (upon the whole) so much steadfastness of purpose, that the more recent foreign policy of England, whether it had been right or whether it had been wrong, was in him almost incarnate. It was obvious, therefore, that whilst he was in the Cabinet he would always be resorted to for counsel upon foreign affairs by any of his colleagues who were not divided from him by strong difference of opinion, by political antagonism, or by personal dislike. Again, it was scarcely wise to believe that the relations which had subsisted between Lord Palmerston and the President of the French Republic would be closed by the fact that they had led to Lord Palmerston's dismissal from the Secretaryship of Foreign Affairs. On the contrary, it was to be inferred that communications of a most friendly kind would continue to pass between the French Emperor and an English Minister who had suffered for his sake; and the very same manliness of disposition which would prevent him from engaging in anything like an underhand intrigue against his colleagues, would make him refuse to sit dumb when, in words brought him fresh from the Tuileries, an ambassador came to talk to him of the Eastern Question, came to tell him that the new Emperor had an unbounded confidence in his judgment, wished to be governed by his counsels, and, in short, would dispose of poor France as the English Minister wished.

Here, then, was the real bridge by which French

overtures of the more secret and delicate sort would come from over the Channel. Here was the bridge by which England's acceptance or rejection of all such overtures would go back to France.

Thus, from the ascendancy of his strong nature, from his vast experience, and from his command of the motive power which he could bring at any moment from Paris, Lord Palmerston, even so early as the spring of 1853, was the most puissant member of Lord Aberdeen's Cabinet; and when, with all these sources of strength, he began to draw support from a people growing every day more and more warlike, he gained a complete dominion. If, after the catastrophe of Sinope, his colleagues had persevered in their attempt to resist him, he would have been able to overthrow them with ease upon the meeting of Parliament.

Therefore, in the transactions which brought on the war, Lord Palmerston was not drifting; he was joyfully laying his course. Whither he meant to go, thither he went; whither he chose that others should tend, thither they bent their reluctant way. If some immortal were to offer the surviving members of Lord Aberdeen's Government the privilege of retracing their steps with all the light of experience, every one of them perhaps, with only a single exception, would examine the official papers of 1853, in order to see where he could most wisely diverge from the course which the Cabinet took.

Lord Palmerston would do nothing of the kind. What he had done before he would do again.

Lord Palmerston's plan of masking the warlike tendency of the Government was an application to politics of an ingenious contrivance, which the Parisians used to employ in some of their street engagements with the soldiery. The contrivance was called a "live barricade." A body of the insurgents would seize the mayor of the arrondissement, and a priest (if they could get one), and also one or two respectable bankers devoted to the cause of peace and order. These prisoners, each forced to walk arm-in-arm between able-bodied combatants, were marched in front of a body of insurgents, which boldly advanced towards a spot where a battalion of infantry might be drawn up in close column of companies; but when they got to within hailing distance, one of the insurgents gifted with a loud voice would shout out to the troops: "Soldiers! respect the cause of "order! Don't fire on Mr. Mayor! Respect property! "Don't level your country's muskets at one who is "a man and a brother, and also a respectable banker! "Soldiers! for the love of God don't imbrue your "hands in the blood of this holy priest!" Confused by this appeal, and shrinking, as was natural, from the duty of killing peaceful citizens, the battalion would hesitate, and meantime the column of the insurgents, covered always by its live barricade, would rapidly advance and crowd in upon the battalion, and break its structure and ruin it. It was thus that Lord Palmerston had the skill to protrude Lord Aberdeen and Mr Gladstone, and keep them standing forward in the van of a Ministry which was bringing the country into war. No one could assail Lord Palmerston's policy without striking at him through men whose conscientious attachment to the cause of peace was beyond the reach of cavil.

In the debates which took place upon the Address, the speeches of the unofficial members of Parliament in both Houses disclosed a strange want of acquaintance with the character and spirit of the negotiations which had been going on for the last eight months. Confiding in the peaceful tendency of a Government headed by Lord Aberdeen, and having Mr Gladstone for one of its foremost members, Mr Bright, in the summer of 1853, had deprecated all discussion; and, under his encouragement, the Government, after some hesitation, determined to withhold the production of the papers. With the lights which he then had, Mr Bright was perhaps entitled to believe that the course he took was the right one, and the intention of the Government was not only honest, but in some degree self-sacrificing; for it cannot be doubted that the disclosure of the able and high-spirited despatches of Lord Clarendon would have raised the Government in public esteem. It is now certain, however, that the disclosure of the papers in the August of 1853 would have enabled the friends of peace to take up a strong ground, to give a new turn to opinion whilst yet there was time, and to save themselves from the utter discomfiture which they underwent in the interval between the prorogation and the meeting of Parliament.

The Cabinet of Lord Aberdeen was not famous for its power of preventing the leakage of State matters; but the common indiscretion by which simple facts are noised abroad does not suffice to disclose the general tenor and bearing of a long and intricate negotiation. Besides, in the absence of means of authentic knowledge, there were circumstances which raised presumptions opposite to the truth. Of course the chief of these was the retention of office by two men whose attachment to the cause of peace was believed to be passionately strong; but it chanced, moreover, that publicity had been given to a highly-spirited and able despatch, the production of the French Foreign Office; and since there had transpired no proof of a corresponding energy on the part of England, it was wrongly inferred that Lord Aberdeen's Government were hanging back. Accordingly, Ministers were taunted for this supposed fault by almost all the speakers in either House. What the Government were chargeable with was an undue forwardness in causing England to join with France alone in the performance of a duty which was European in its nature, and devolving in the first instance upon Austria. What they were charged with was a want of readiness to do that which they had done. Therefore every one who spoke against the Ministry was committing himself to opinions which (as soon as their real course of action should be disclosed) would involve him in an approval of their policy.

Production of the Papers.

But now at last, and within a day or two from the conclusion of the debate on the Address, some of the papers relating to the negotiations of 1853 and the preceding years were laid upon the table of both Houses. As soon as the more devoted friends of peace were able to read these documents, and in some degree to comprehend their scope and bearing, they began to see how their cause had fared under the official guardianship of Lord Aberdeen and Mr Gladstone. They began to see that for near eight months the Government had been following a course of action which was gently leading towards war. They did not, however, make out the way in which the deflection began. They did not see that the way in which the Government had lapsed from the paths of peace, was by quitting the common ground of the four Powers for the sake of a closer union with one, and by joining with the French Emperor in making a perverse use of the fleets.

Their effect.

Mr Cobden fastened upon the "Vienna Note," and, with his views, he was right in drawing attention to the apparent narrowness of the difference upon which the question of peace or war was made to depend; but he surely betrayed a want of knowledge of the way in which the actions of mankind are governed when he asked that a country now glowing with warlike ardour should go back and try to obtain peace by resuming a form of words which its Government had solemnly repudiated four months before. Of course this effort failed: it could not be otherwise. Any one acquainted with the tenor of the negotiations, and with enough of the surrounding facts to make the papers intelligible, may be able to judge whether there were not better grounds than this for making a stand against the war. The evil demanding redress was the intrusion of the Russian forces into Wallachia and Moldavia; and it would seem that the judgment to be pronounced by Parliament upon a Government which had led their country to the brink of war should have been made to depend upon this question:—

CHAP. XXVI.

Was it practicable for England to obtain the deliverance of the Principalities by means taken in common with the rest of the four Powers, and without resorting to the expedient of a separate understanding with the French Emperor?

The question on which the judgment of Parliament should have been rested.

It may be that to this question the surviving members of Lord Aberdeen's Administration can establish a negative answer, but in order to do this they will have to make use of knowledge not hitherto disclosed to Parliament.

A belief, nay, even a suspicion, that there was danger of a sudden alliance between the French Emperor and the Czar, would gravely alter the conditions upon which Lord Aberdeen's Cabinet was called upon to form its judgment; but, so far as the outer world knows, no fear of this kind was coercing the Government. Upon the papers as they stand, it seems clear that, by remaining upon the ground occupied by the four Powers, England would have obtained the deliverance of the Principalities without resorting to war.

CHAPTER XXVII.

THE last of the steps which brought on the final rupture between Russia and the Western Powers was perhaps one of the most anomalous transactions which the annals of diplomacy have recorded. The outrage to be redressed was the occupation by Russia of Wallachia and Moldavia. Of all the States of Europe, except Turkey itself, the one most aggrieved by this occupation was Austria. Now Austria was one of the great Powers of Europe. She was essentially a military State; she was the mistress of a vast and well-appointed army; she was the neighbour of Russia. Geographically, she was so placed that (whatever perils she might bring upon her other frontiers) her mere order to her officer commanding her army of observation would necessarily force the Czar to withdraw his troops. On the other hand, France and England, though justly offended by the outrage, and though called upon in their character as two of the great Powers to concur in fit measures for suppressing it, were far from being brought into any grievous stress by the occupation of the far-distant Principalities; and moreover, the evil, such

CHAP. XXVII.

Austria proposes that France and England should summon the Czar to quit the Principalities, and threaten war as the result of his refusal.

as it was, was one which they could not dispel by any easy or simple application of force.

It was in this condition of things that Austria suddenly conveyed to France, and through France to England, the intimation of the 22d of February. In conversation with Baron de Bourqueney, Count Buol said: "If England and France will fix a day "for the evacuation of the Principalities, the expira- "tion of which shall be the signal for hostilities, the "Cabinet of Vienna will support the summons."* The telegraph conveyed the tenor of this intimation to London on the same day. Naturally, it was to be expected that Austria would join in a summons which she invited other Powers to send; and to this hour it seems hardly possible to believe that the Emperor of Austria deliberately intended to ask France and England to fix a day for going to war without meaning to go to war himself at the same time. Lord Clarendon, however, asked the question. Apparently he was not answered in terms corresponding with his question, but he was again told that Austria would "support" the summons. Then, all at once, and without stipulating for the concurrence of the Power which was pressing them into action, the Governments of France and England prepared the instruments which were to bring them into a state of war with Russia.

Austria at this period had plainly resolved to go

---

* "Eastern Papers," part vii. p. 53.

to war if the Principalities should not be relinquished by the Czar; but, before she could take the final step, it was necessary for her to come to an understanding with Prussia. This she succeeded in doing within twenty-four days from the period of the final rupture between Russia and the Western Powers; but France and England could not bear to wait. The French Emperor, rebuffed by the Czar in his endeavour to appear as the pacificator of Europe, was driven to the opposite method of diverting France from herself; and although the crisis was one in which a little delay and a little calmness would have substituted the coercive action of the four Powers for an adventurous war by the two, he once more goaded our Government on, and pressed it into instant action. M. Drouyn de Lhuys declared that, in his opinion, the sending of the proposed summons was a business which "should be done immediately, and that the "two Governments should write to Count Nesselrode "to demand the immediate" withdrawal of the Russian troops from the Principalities — "the whole to "be concluded by a given time, say the end of "March."* It must be owned, however, that the English people were pressing their Government in the same direction. Inflamed with a longing for naval glory in the Baltic, they had become tormented with a fear lest their Admiral should be hindered from great achievements for want of the mere legal for-

CHAP. XXVII.

Importance of avoiding haste.

Pressure of the French Emperor.

Eagerness of the people in England.

---

* "Eastern Papers," part vii. p. 53.

mality which was to constitute a state of war. The majority of the Cabinet, though numbering on their side several of the foremost statesmen of the day, were collectively too weak to help being driven by the French Emperor, too weak to help being infected by the warlike eagerness of the people, too weak to resist the strong man who was amongst them without being of them. It is likely enough that statesmen so gifted as some of them were, must have had better grounds for their way of acting than have been hitherto disclosed; but to one who only judges from the materials communicated to Parliament, it seems plain that at this time they had lost their composure.

By the summons despatched on the part of England, Lord Clarendon informed Count Nesselrode that unless the Russian Government, within six days from the delivery of the summons, should send an answer engaging to withdraw all its troops from the Principalities by the 30th of April, its refusal or omission so to do would be regarded by England as a declaration of war. This summons was in accordance with the suggestion of Austria; and what might have been expected was, that the Western Powers, in acceding to her wish, should do so upon the understanding that she concurred in the measure which she herself proposed, and that they would consult her as to the day on which it would be convenient for her to enter into a state of war; in other words, that they would consult her as to the day on which a continued refusal to quit the Principalities should bring the Czar into a state of war with Austria, France, and England. Instead of taking this course, Lord Clarendon forwarded the summons (not as a draft or project, but as a document already signed and complete) to the Court of Vienna, and it was despatched by a messenger, who (after remaining for only a "few hours" in the Austrian capital) was to carry on the summons to St Petersburg. Therefore Austria was made aware that, whether she was willing to defend her own interests or not, England was irrevocably committed to defend them for her; and instead of requiring that Austria should take part in the step which she herself had advised, Lord Westmorland was merely instructed to express a hope that the summons "would meet with the approval" of the Austrian Cabinet, and that their opinion of it would be made known by Count Buol to the Cabinet of St Petersburg. Such a step as this on the part of Austria was preposterously short of what the Western Powers would have had a right to expect from her, if they had been a little less eager for hostilities, and had consulted her as to the time for coming to a rupture.

Of course the impatience of France and England was ruinous to the principle of maintaining concert between the four Powers; and what made it the more lamentable was, that it did not spring from any sound military views. It is true that the Western Powers were sending troops to the Levant and fitting out fleets for the Baltic; but there was nothing in the

CHAP. XXVII.

The counter-proposals of Russia reach Vienna at the same time as the English messenger.

They are rejected by the Conference of the four Powers.

Austria and Prussia "support" the summons, but without taking part in the step.

state of their preparations, nor in the position of the respective forces, which could justify their eagerness to accelerate the declaration of war.

It chanced that, simultaneously with the arrival of the English messenger at Vienna, there came thither from St Petersburg the counter-propositions of Russia. Count Buol saw the importance of disposing of these before the summons went on to St Petersburg; so, after persuading Lord Westmorland to detain the English messenger, he instantly assembled the Conference of the four Powers. By this Conference the counter-propositions of Russia were unanimously rejected,* and the bearer of the summons carried this decision of the four Powers to St Petersburg, together with a despatch from the Austrian Government, instructing Count Esterhazy to support the summons, and throwing upon Russia the responsibility of the impending war.** The despatch, however, fell short of announcing that the refusal to quit the Principalities would place the Czar in a state of war with Austria as well as with the Western Powers. Prussia supported the summons in language corresponding with the language of the Vienna Cabinet. Baron Manteuffel's despatch to St Petersburg "was drawn up in very pressing lan-"guage. It urged the Russian Government to con-

---

* "The Conference unanimously agreed that it was impossible "to proceed with those propositions." — Protocol of Conference of March 5. "Eastern Papers," part vii. p. 80.

** "Eastern Papers," part vii. p. 64.

"sider the dangers to which the peace of the world
"would be exposed by a refusal, and declared that
"the responsibility of the war which might be the
"consequence of that refusal would rest with the
"Emperor."*

The summons addressed by France to the Russian Government was in the same terms as the summons despatched by Lord Clarendon, and was forwarded at the same time.

After receiving the summons of the two Governments, Count Nesselrode took the final orders of his master, and then informed the Consuls of France and England that the Emperor did not think fit to send any answer to their Notes. A refusal to answer was one of the events which, under the terms of the announcement contained in the summons, was to be regarded by the Western Powers as a declaration of war. This refusal was uttered by Count Nesselrode on the 19th of March 1854. The peace between the great Powers of Europe had lasted more than thirty-eight years, and now at length it was broken.

On the 27th of March a message from the Emperor of the French informed his Senate and Legislative Assembly that the last determination of the Cabinet of St Petersburg had placed France and Russia in a state of war. In his speech from the throne at the opening of the session** he had already

* "Eastern Papers," part vii. p. 72.
** March 2.

declared that war was upon the point of commencing. "To avoid a conflict," he said, "I have gone as far "as honour allowed. Europe now knows that if "France draws the sword it is because she is con- "strained to do so. Europe knows that France has "no idea of aggrandisement; she only wishes to "resist dangerous encroachments. The time of con- "quests has passed away, never to return. This "policy has had for its result a more intimate alliance "between England and France." It is curious to observe that only a few hours after the time when England became inextricably engaged with him in a joint war against Russia, and in the same speech in which he announced the fact, the French Emperor acknowledged the value and the practicability of the wholesome policy which he had just then superseded by drawing the Cabinet of London into a separate alliance with himself; but when he was declaring, in words already quoted, that "Germany had re- "covered her political independence, that Austria "would enter into the alliance, and that the Western "Powers would go to Constantinople along with "Germany," he had the happiness of knowing that the baneful summons which was to bring France and England into a separate course of action, and place them at last in a state of war, had been signed by the English Minister for Foreign Affairs, and was already on the way to St Petersburg.*

* The messenger had reached Berlin on the day of the French Emperor's Speech from the throne.

On the same 27th of March a message from the Queen announced to Parliament that the negotiations with Russia were broken off, and that her Majesty, feeling bound to give active aid to the Sultan, relied upon the efforts of her faithful subjects to aid her in protecting the states of the Sultan against the encroachments of Russia. On the following day the English declaration of war was issued. The labour of putting into writing the grounds for a momentous course of action is a wholesome discipline for statesmen; and it would be well for mankind if, at a time when the question were really in suspense, the friends of a policy leading towards war were obliged to come out of the mist of oral intercourse and private notes, and to put their view into a firm piece of writing. It does not follow that such a document ought necessarily to be disclosed, but it ought to exist, and it ought to be official. In the summer of 1853 the draft of a document, fairly stating the grounds of that singular policy of alliance within alliance which was shadowed out in the Royal Speech at the close of the session, would have been a good exercise for the members of Lord Aberdeen's Cabinet, and would have protected them against that sensation of "drifting," which was afterwards described by the Foreign Secretary. It is known that when the English declaration announcing the rupture with Russia was about to be prepared, it was found less easy than might be supposed to assign reasons for the war. The necessity of having

CHAP. XXVII.
Difficulty of framing it.

to state the cause of the rupture in a solemn and precise form, disclosed the vice of the policy which the Government was following; for it could not be concealed that the grievance which was inducing France and England to take up arms was one of an European kind, which called for redress at the hands of the four Powers rather than for the armed championship of the two.

Of course the difficulty was overcome. When the faith of the country was pledged, and fleets and armies already moving to the scene of the conflict, it was not possible that war would be stayed for want of mere words. The Queen was advised to declare, that, by the regard due to an ally, and to an empire whose integrity and independence were essential to the peace of Europe, by the sympathies of her people for the cause of right against injustice, and from a desire to save Europe from the preponderance of a Power which had violated the faith of treaties, she felt called upon to take up arms, in concert with the Emperor of the French, for the defence of the Sultan.

The Czar's declaration and War manifesto.

On the 11th of April the Emperor of Russia issued his declaration of war. He declared that the summons addressed to him by France and England took from Russia all possibility of yielding with honour; and he threw the responsibility of the war upon the Western Powers. It was for Central and Western Europe that diplomacy shaped these phrases; but in the manifesto addressed to his own people the Czar used loftier words. "Russia," said he, "fights "not for the things of this world, but for the Faith."* "England and France have ranged themselves by the "side of the enemies of Christianity against Russia "fighting for the Orthodox faith. But Russia will "not alter her divine mission; and if enemies fall "upon her frontier, we are ready to meet them with "the firmness which our ancestors have bequeathed "to us. Are we not now the same Russian nation of "whose deeds of valour the memorable events of 1812 "bear witness? May the Almighty assist us to prove "this by deeds! And in this trust taking up arms "for our persecuted brethren professing the Christian "faith, we will exclaim with the whole of Russia with "one heart, 'O Lord our Saviour, whom have we "'to fear?' 'May God arise and His enemies be "'dispersed!'"**

On the fourth day after the delivery of the message which placed Russia in a state of war with France and England, Prince Gortschakoff passed the Lower Danube at three points, and, entering into the desolate region of the Dobrudja, began the invasion of Turkey.***

* 23d April.
** 21st February.
*** 24th March. By thus passing that part of the river which encloses the Dobrudja, a general does not effect much. He must cross it at and above Rassova before he can be said, in the military sense, to have "broken through the line of the Danube."

CHAP. XXVII.
Treaty between the Sultan and the Western Powers.

Nearly at the same time France and England entered into a treaty with the Sultan, by which they engaged to defend Turkey with their arms until the conclusion of a peace guaranteeing the independence of the Ottoman Empire and the rights of the Sultan, and upon the close of the war to withdraw all their forces from the Ottoman territory. The Sultan, on his part, undertook to make no separate peace or armistice with Russia.*

Treaty between France and England.

On the 10th of April 1854 there was signed that treaty of alliance between France and England which many men had suffered themselves to look upon as a security for the peace of Europe. The high contracting parties engaged to do what lay in their power for the re-establishment of a peace which should secure Europe against the return of the existing troubles; and in order to set free the Sultan's dominions, they promised to use all the land and sea forces required for the purpose. They engaged to receive no overture tending to the cessation of hostilities, and to enter into no engagement with the Russian Court, without having deliberated in common. They renounced all aim at separate advantages, and they declared their readiness to receive into their alliance any of the other Powers of Europe.

* 10th of March.

CHAP. XXVIII.

This great alliance did not carry with it so resistless a weight as to be able to execute justice by its own sheer force, and without the shedding of blood; but it was a mighty engine of war.

CHAPTER XXVIII.

CHAP. XXVIII. Recapitulation.

Standing causes of disturbance.

Effect of personal government by the Czar.

The train of causes which brought on the war has now been followed down to the end. Great armies kept on foot, and empires governed by princes without the counsel of statesmen, were spoken of in the outset as standing elements of danger to the cause of peace; and their bearing upon the disputes of nations has been seen in all the phases of a strife which began in a quarrel for a key and a trinket, and ended by embroiling Europe. Upon the destinies of Russia the effect of this system of mere personal government has been seen at every step. From head to foot a vast empire was made to throb with the passions which rent the bosom of the one man Nicholas. If for a few months he harboured ambition, the resources of the State were squandered in making ready for war. If his spirit flagged, the ambition of the State fell lame, and preparations ceased. If he laboured under a fit of piety, or rather of ecclesiastic zeal, All the Russias were on the verge of a crusade. He chafed with rage at the thought of being foiled in diplomatic strife by the second Canning; and instantly, without hearing counsel from any living man, he caused his docile battalions to cross the frontier, and kindled a bloody war.

CHAP. XXVIII.

Nor was the personal government of the Emperor Francis Joseph without its share of mischief; for it seems clear that this was the evil course by which Austria was brought into measures offensive to the Sultan, but full of danger to herself. More than once, in the autumn of 1852, Nicholas and Francis Joseph came together; and at these ill-omened meetings, the youthful Kaiser, bending, it would seem, under a weight of gratitude — overwhelmed by the personal ascendancy of the Czar — and touched, as he well might be, by the affection which Nicholas had conceived for him—was led perhaps to use language which never would have been sanctioned by a cabinet of Austrian statesmen; and although it is understood that he abstained from actual promises, it is hard to avoid believing that the general tenor of the young Emperor's conversations with Nicholas must have been the chief cause which led the Czar to imagine that he could enter upon a policy highly dangerous to Austria, and yet safely count upon her assent. The Czar never could have hoped that Austrian councillors of state would have willingly stood still and endured his seizure of the country of the Lower Danube from Orsova down to the Euxine; but he understood that Francis Joseph governed Austria, and he imagined that he could govern Francis Joseph as though he

By the Emperor of Austria.

were his own child. "He could reckon," he said, "upon Austria."*

<small>CHAP. XXVIII.</small>

<small>By the King of Prussia.</small>
Even in Prussia the policy of the State seemed to be always upon the point of being shaken by the fears of the King; and although, up to the outbreak of the war, she was guilty of no defection,** it is certain that the anticipation of finding weakness in this quarter was one of the causes which led the Czar into danger.

<small>By the French Emperor.</small>
In France, after the events of the 2d of December, the system of personal government so firmly obtained, that the narrator — dispensed from the labour of inquiring what interests she had in the question of peace and war, and what were the thoughts of her orators, her statesmen, and her once illustrious writers — was content to see what scheme of action would best conduce to the welfare and safety of a small knot of men then hanging together in Paris; and when it appeared that, upon the whole, these persons would gain in safety and comfort from the disturbance of Europe, and from a close understanding with England, the subsequent progress of the story was singularly unembarrassed by any question about what might be the policy demanded

---

* Memorandum by the Emperor of Russia, delivered to the English Government *ubi anis.*

** It was more than three months after the outbreak of the war that Prussia halted.

by the interests or the sentiments of France. Therefore the bearing of personal government upon the maintenance of peace was better illustrated by the French Government than by the Emperor Nicholas; for in the Czar, after all, a vast people was incarnate. His ambition, his piety, his anger, were in a sense the passions of the devoted millions of men of whom he was indeed the true chief. The French Emperor, on the contrary, when he chose to carry France into a war against Russia, was in no respect the champion of a national policy nor of a national sentiment; and he therefore gave a vivid example of the way in which sheer personal government comes to bear upon the peace of the world.

CHAP. XXVIII.

Perhaps if a man were to undertake to distribute the blame of the war, the first Power he would arraign might be Russia. Her ambition, her piety, and her Church zeal were ancient causes of strife, which were kindled into a dangerous activity by the question of the Sanctuaries, and by events which seemed for a moment to show that the time for her favourite enterprise against Constantinople might now at last be coming. Until the month of March 1853, these causes were brought to bear directly against the tranquillity of Europe; and even after that time they were in one sense the parents of strife, because, though they ceased to have a direct action upon events, they had set other forces in motion. But it would be wrong to believe that, after the

Share which Russia had in bringing about the War.

middle of March 1853, Russia was acting in furtherance of any scheme of territorial aggrandisement; for it is plain that by that time the Czar's vague ambition had dwindled down into a mere wish to wring from the Porte a protectorate of the Greek Church in Turkey. He had gathered his troops upon the Turkish frontier, and it seemed to him that he could use their presence there as a means of extorting an engagement which would soothe the pride of the Orthodox Church, and tighten the rein by which he was always seeking to make the Turks feel his power. The vain concealments and misrepresentations by which this effort of violent diplomacy was accompanied, were hardly worthy to be ranked as acts of statecraft, and were rather the discord produced by the clashing impulses of a mind in conflict with itself.

Originally the Czar had no thought of going to war for the sake of obtaining this engagement, and least of all had he any thought of going to war with England. At first he thought to obtain it by surprise; and, when that attempt failed, he still hoped to obtain it by resolute pressure, because he reckoned that if the great Powers would compare the slenderness of the required concession with the evils of a great war, there could be no question how they would choose.

As soon as the diplomatic strife at Constantinople began to work, the Czar got heated by it; and when at length he found himself not only contending for his Church, but contending too with his ancient enemy, he so often lost all self-command, that what he did in his politic intervals was never enough to undo the evil which he wrought in his fits of pious zeal and of rage. And when, with a cruel grace, and before the eyes of all Europe, Lord Stratford disposed of Prince Mentschikoff, it must be owned that it was hard for a proud man in the place of the Czar to have to stand still and submit. Therefore, without taking counsel of any man, he resolved to occupy the Principalities; but he had no belief that even that grave step would involve him in war; for his dangerous faith in Lord Aberdeen and in the power of the English Peace Party was in full force, and grew to a joyful and ruinous certainty when he learned that the Queen's Prime Minister had insisted upon revoking the grave words which had been uttered to Baron Brunnow by the Secretary of State. This illusory faith in the peacefulness of England long continued to be his guide; and from time to time he was confirmed in his choice of the wrong path by the bearing of the persons who represented France, Austria, and Prussia at the Court of St Petersburg; for although in Paris, in London, in Vienna, in Berlin, and in Constantinople the four great Powers seemed strictly united in their desire to restrain the encroachments of the Czar, this wholesome concord was so masked at St Petersburg by the demeanour of Count Mensdorf, Colonel Rochow, and M. Castelbajac, that Sir Hamilton Seymour, though uttering the known opinion of the other three Powers as well as of his own Government, was left to stand alone.

After his acceptance of the Vienna Note, the Emperor Nicholas enjoyed for a few days the bliss of seeing all Europe united with him against the Turks, and he believed perhaps that Heaven was favouring him once more, and that now at last "Can- "ning" was vanquished; but in a little while the happy dream ceased, and he had the torment of hearing the four Powers confess that, if for a moment they had differed from Lord Stratford, it was because of their erring nature. Then, fired by the Turkish declaration of war, and stung to fury by the hostile use of the Western fleets which the French Emperor had forced upon the English Government, the Czar gave the fatal orders which brought about the disaster of Sinope. After his first exultation over the sinking of the ships and the slaughter, he apparently saw his error, and was become so moderate as to receive in a right spirit the announcement of the first decision that had been taken by the English Cabinet when the news of the catastrophe reached it. But only a few days later he had to hear of the grave and hostile change of view which had been forced upon Lord Aberdeen's Government by the French Emperor, and to learn that, by resolving to drive the Russian flag from the Euxine, the maritime Powers had brought their relations with his empire to a state barely short of war. After this rupture it was no longer possible for him to extricate himself decorously, unless by exerting some skill and a steady command of temper. He was unequal to the trial; and although, in politic and worldly moments, he must have been almost hopeless of a good result, he could not bear to let go his hold of the occupied provinces under the compulsion of a public threat laid upon him by England and France.

CHAP.
XXVIII.

With the conduct of the **Turkish Government** little fault is to be found. It is true that, in the early stage of the dispute about the Sanctuaries, the violence of the French and the Russian Governments tormented the Porte into contradictory engagements, and that the anger kindled by these clashing promises was one of the provocatives of the war; but from the day of the delivery of the Bethlehem key and the replacement of the star, the Turkish Government was almost always moderate and politic — and after the second week of March 1853 it was firm; for the panic struck by Prince Mentschikoff in the early days of his mission was allayed by the prudent boldness of Colonel Rose, and the Czar with all his hovering forces was never able to create a second alarm.

Share which Turkey had in causing it.

It has been seen that, by their tenacity of all those sovereign rights which were of real worth — by the wisdom with which they yielded wherever they could yield with honour and safety — by their invincible courtesy and deference towards their mighty assailant — and at last, and above all, by their warlike ardour and their prowess in the field — the Turks had become an example to Christendom, and had won the heart of England. And although it has been acknowledged that some of the more gentle of these Turkish virtues were contrived and enforced by the English Ambassador, still no one can fairly refuse to the Ottoman people the merit of appreciating and enduring this painful discipline.

Besides, there was a period when it might be supposed that the immediate views of the Turkish Government and of the English Ambassador were not exactly the same; for as soon as the Turkish statesmen became aware that their appeal to the people had kindled a spirit which was forcing them into war, it of course became their duty to endeavour to embroil the other Powers of Europe; and they laboured in this direction with much sagacity and skill. They saw that if they could contrive to bring up the Admirals from Besika Bay, the Western Powers would soon get decoyed into war by their own fleets; and in order to this, we saw Reshid Pasha striving to affect the lofty mind of Lord Stratford by shadowing out the ruin of the Ottoman dominion; then mounting his horse, going off to the French Ambassador, and so changing the elevation of his soul, whilst he rode from one Embassy to the other, that in the presence of M. de la Cour he no longer spoke of a falling empire, but pictured to him a crowd of Frenchmen of all ranks cruelly massacred, on account of their well-known Christianity, by a host of fanatical Moslems. And although the serenity of Lord Stratford defeated the sagacious Turk for the time, and disappointed him in his endeavour to bring up more than a couple of vessels from each fleet, still in the end the Turkish statesmanship prevailed; for M. de la Cour, disturbed by the bloody prospect held out to him, communicated his excitement to the French Emperor, and the French Emperor, as we have seen, then put so hard a pressure upon Lord Aberdeen as to constrain him to join in breaking through the treaty of 1841; and since this resolve led straight into the series of naval movements which followed, and so on to the outbreak of war, the members of the Sultan's Cabinet had some right to believe that, even without the counsels of the great Ambassador, they knew how to govern events.

In so far as the origin of the war was connected with Count Leiningen's mission, Austria is answerable; and although it must needs be true (for so she firmly declares*) that the Czar's reiterated account

---

* I have a statement to this effect. To those who have not been called upon to test the relative worth of statements coming from different parts of Europe, it may seem that I am facile in accepting this one; and the more so when I acknowledge, as I do, that surrounding

of his close understanding with her in regard to Montenegro was purely fabulous, she still remains open to the grave charge of having sent Count Leiningen to Constantinople armed with a long string of questionable claims, yet debarred by his orders from all negotiation, and instructed to receive no answer from the Turkish Government except an answer of simple consent or simple refusal. This offensive method of pressing upon an independent Sovereign was constantly referred to by the Czar as justifying and almost compelling his determination to deal with the Sultan in a high-handed fashion; and in this way (even upon the supposition of there being no pernicious understanding between the two Emperors) Count Leiningen's mission had an ill effect upon the maintenance of peace.

Again, Austria must bear the blame of employing servants who, notwithstanding the firm and right part which she took in the negotiations, were always causing her to appear before Europe as a Power subservient to the Czar; and especially she ought to suffer in public repute for the effect produced at St Petersburg by her representative's shameful presence

---

facts give an appearance of probability to the opposite assertion. The truth is that, like our own countrymen, the public men of Austria are much accustomed to subordinate their zeal for the public service to their self-respect. To undertake to disbelieve a statesman of the Court of Vienna, is the same thing as to undertake to disbelieve an English gentleman.

at the thanksgivings which the Czar and his people offered up to the Almighty for the sinking of the ships and the slaughter of the Turks at Sinope.

There is also a fault of omission for which it would seem that Austria is chargeable. The interests of Austria and England, both present and remote, were so strictly the same, that for the welfare of both States there ought to have been going on between them a constant interchange of friendly counsels. Our statesmen are accustomed to proffer advice without stint to foreign States, but it is remarkable that their frankness is not much reciprocated by words of friendly counsel from abroad. Yet there are times when such counsels might be wholesome. It would surely have been well if Austria had advised the English Government not to quit the safe, honest ground held by the four Powers, for the sake of an adventure with the new Bonaparte. There is no trace of any such warnings from Vienna; and indeed it would seem that Austria, tormented by the presence of the Russian forces on her southern frontier, was more prone to encourage than to restrain the imprudence of her old ally.

These were the faults with which Austria may fairly be charged. In other respects she was not forgetful of her duty towards herself and towards Europe; and it has been seen that, from the day when the Czar crossed the Pruth down to the time when he was obliged to relinquish his hold, Austria

In other respects Austria discharged her duty.

CHAP. XXVIII.

Share which Prussia had in causing the War.

persisted in taking the same view of the dispute as was taken by the Western Powers, and was never at all backward in her measures for the deliverance of the Principalities.

In the nature and temperament of the King of Prussia there was so much of weakness that his Imperial brother-in-law was accustomed to speak of him in terms of ruthless disdain; and it seems that this habit of looking down upon the King caused the Czar to shape his policy simply as though Prussia were null. When he found his Royal brother-in-law engaged against him in an offensive and defensive alliance, he perhaps understood the error which he had committed in assuming that the policy of an enlightened and a high-spirited nation would be steadily subservient to the weakness of its Sovereign; but until he was thus undeceived, or, at all events, until the failure of Baron Budberg's mission in the beginning of 1854, he seems to have closed his eyes to all the long series of public acts in which Prussia had engaged, and to have cheated himself into the belief that she would never take up such a ground as might enable Austria to act freely on her southern frontier, and so drive him out of the Principalities. And, although until after the outbreak of the war between Russia and the Western Powers Prussia did not at all hang back,[*] it is nevertheless

---

[*] The state of war began on the 19th of March. Prussia first began to hang back about the 21st of July. See *ante*.

true that the Czar's policy was shaped upon a knowledge of the King's weak nature. Therefore the temperament and mental quality of the Prussian monarch must be reckoned among the causes of the war.

Prussia also in the same degree as Austria must bear the kind of repute that was entailed upon her by the conduct of her representative; his thanksgiving for the slaughter of Sinope will long be remembered against her.

Another fault attributable to Prussia was her invincible love of metaphysical or rather mere verbal refinements. When this form of human error is brought into politics it chills all human sympathies, and tends to bring a country into contempt, by giving to its policy the bitter taste of a theory or a doctrine, and so causing it to be misunderstood. An instance of this vice was given by the First Minister of the Prussian Crown, in a speech of great moment which he addressed to the Lower Chamber on the 18th of March 1854. After an abundance of phrases of a pacific tendency, Baron Manteuffel said that Prussia was resolved "faithfully to aid "any member of the Confederation who, from his "geographical position, might feel himself called "upon sooner than Prussia to draw the sword in "defence of German interests." Now this, to the ear of any diplomatist, foreshadowed, or rather announced, an offensive and defensive alliance with Austria against

CHAP. XXVIII.

the Czar for the delivery of the Principalities; and accordingly, the alliance so announced was actually contracted by Prussia some four weeks afterwards. But, in the minds of the common public, a disclosure couched in this diplomatic phraseology was smothered under the intolerable weight of the pacific verbiage which had gone before; and the result was, that a speech which announced a measure of offence and hostility to Russia was looked upon as the disclosure of a halting, timid, and worthless policy.

In other respects Prussia discharged her duty.

But, except upon the grounds here stated, there was no grave fault to find with the policy of Prussia down to the outbreak of the war between the Czar and the Western Powers. Distant as she was from the scene of the Czar's encroachment, she was nevertheless compelled, as she valued her hold upon the goodwill of Germany, to be steadfast in hindering Russia from establishing herself in provinces which would give her the full control of the Lower Danube; and up to the time of the final rupture she always so accommodated her policy to the views of the Western Powers as to be able to remain in firm accord with them, both as to the adjudication of the dispute between Russia and Turkey, and as to the principles which should guide the belligerents in the event of their being forced into a war by the obstinacy of the Emperor Nicholas.

Of course the Czar's relinquishment of the Principalities took away from Prussia, as well as from Austria, her ground of complaint against the Czar, and with it her motive for action. Nor was this all; for by determining to quit the mainland of Europe and make a descent upon a remote maritime province of Russia, the Western Powers deprived themselves of all right to expect that Austria and Prussia would favour a scheme of invasion which they did not and could not approve. Down to the time when the Czar determined to repass the Pruth, the policy followed by Prussia, as well as by Austria, was sound and loyal towards Europe.

<small>CHAP. XXVIII.</small>

The German Confederation was brought into the same views as Austria and Prussia; and thus, so long as the object in view was the deliverance of the Principalities, the whole of Central Europe was joined with the great Powers of the West in a determination to repress the Czar's encroachments. I repeat that the papers laid before the Parliament have not yet disclosed the ground on which the English Government became discontent with this vast union, and was led to contract those separate engagements with the Emperor of the French which ended by bringing on the war.

<small>As did also the German Confederation.</small>

The blame of beginning the dispute which led on to the war must rest with the French Government; for it is true, as our Foreign Secretary declared, that "the Ambassador of France at Constantinople was the first to disturb the status quo

<small>Share which the French Government had in causing the War.</small>

"in which the matter rested, and without political "action on the part of France, the quarrels of the "Churches would never have troubled the relations "of friendly Powers."* For this offence against the tranquillity of Europe the President of the Republic was answerable in the first instance; but it must be remembered that at the time France was under a free-Parliamentary Government; and it is just, therefore, to acknowledge that the blame of sanctioning the disinterment of a forgotten treaty more than a hundred years old, and of violently using it as an instrument of disturbance, must be shared by an Assembly which had not enough of the statesmanlike quality to be able to denounce a wanton and noxious policy. It was the weakness of the gifted statesmen and orators who then adorned the Chambers that, like most of their countrymen, they were too easily fascinated by the pleasure of seeing France domineer.

But at the close of the year 1851 the France known to Europe and the world was bereaved of political life; and thenceforth her complex interests in the affairs of nations were so effectually overruled by the exigency of personal considerations, that in a little while she was made to adopt an Anglo-Turkish policy, and, as the price of this concession to the views of our Foreign Office, the venturers of the 2d of December were brought under the sanctions

* *Ubi ante.*

of an alliance with the Queen of England. It has been seen that, by superseding that conjoint action of the four Powers which was the true safeguard of peace and justice, the separate compact of the two became a main cause of the appeal to arms. Moreover, it has been shown how, when once he had entangled Lord Aberdeen's Government in this understanding, the French Emperor gained so strong a hold over it that he became able to guide and overrule the counsels of England even in the use to be made of her Mediterranean fleet; and how thenceforth, and from time to time, he so used the English navy as well as his own, that at the moments when the negotiations seemed ripe for peace they were always defeated by an order sent out to the Admirals. The real tendency of this perturbing and dislocating course of action was concealed by the moderation which characterised the French despatches, and, in another and very different way, by the demeanour of the personage who represented the French Government at St Petersburg; so that, at the very times when Lord Aberdeen was brought to consent to a hostile and provoking use of our naval forces, he was able to derive fatal comfort from the language of the French diplomacy; and whenever the grave tone of Sir Hamilton Seymour was beginning to produce wholesome effect at St Petersburg, his efforts were quickly baffled by the prostrations of his French colleague.

CHAP.
XXVIII.

It was thus that, by generating the original dispute — by drawing England from the common ground of the four Powers into a separate understanding with himself — by causing a persistently hostile use to be made of the fleets, and, finally, by his ambiguous ways of speaking and acting — the French Emperor came to have a chief share in the kindling of the war.

Share which England had in causing it.

The stake which England holds in the world makes it of deep moment to her to avert disorder among nations; and, on the other hand, her insular station in Europe, joined with the possession of more than sufficing empire in other regions of the world, keeps her clear of all thought of territorial aggrandisement in this quarter of the globe. And although it is the duty of all the rest of the great Powers as well as of England to endeavour towards the maintenance of peace and order, yet, inasmuch as there is no other great State without some sort of lurking ambition which may lead it into temptation, the fidelity of the Continental guardians of the peace can always be brought into question. Suspicions of this kind are often fanciful, but the fears from which they spring are too well founded in the nature of things to be safely regarded as frivolous; and the result is, that the great island Power is the one which, by the well-informed statesmen of the Continent, is looked to as the surest safeguard against wrong. Europe leans, Europe rests, on this faith.

So, the moment it is made to appear that for any reason England is disposed to abdicate, or to suspend for a while, the performance of her European duties, that moment the wrong-doer sees his opportunity and begins to stir. Those who dread him, missing the accustomed safeguard of England, turn whither they can for help, and, failing better plans of safety, they perhaps try hard to make terms with the spoiler. Monarchs find that to conspire for gain of territory, or to have other princes conspiring against them, is the alternative presented to their choice. The system of Europe becomes decomposed, and war follows. Therefore, exactly in proportion as England values the peace of Europe, she ought to abstain from every word and from every sign which tends to give the wrong-doer a hope of her acquiescence. Unhappily this duty was not understood by the more ardent friends of peace; and they imagined that they would serve their cause by entreating England to abstain from every conflict which did not menace their own shores—nay, even by permitting themselves to vow and declare that this was the policy truly loved by the English race. Moreover, by blending their praises of peace with fierce invective against public men, they easily drew applause from assembled multitudes, and so caused the foreigner to believe that they really spoke the voice of a whole people, or at all events of great masses, and that England was no longer a Power which would interfere with spoliation in Europe. The fatal effect which this belief produced upon the peace of Europe has been shown. But the evil produced by the excesses of the Peace Party did not end there. It is the nature of excesses to beget excesses of strange complexion; and just as a too rigid sanctity has always been followed by a too scandalous profligacy, so, by the law of reaction, the doctrines of the Peace Party tended to bring into violent life that keen warlike spirit which soon became one of the main obstacles to the restoration of tranquillity. Therefore England, it must be acknowledged, did much to bring on the war; first, by the want of moderation and prudence with which she seemed to declare her attachment to the cause of peace — and afterwards by the exceeding eagerness with which she coveted the strife.

We have seen the steps by which England was brought from her seeming peacefulness into a temper impatiently warlike; but, considering the much-avowed attachment of England to the maintenance of peace — the indirect, not to say remote, way in which the Eastern dispute came to bear upon English interests — and, on the other hand, the immense concurrence of opinion which sanctioned and at last almost compelled the appeal to arms, — it is hard at first sight to understand how it came to happen that the cause of peace was, not merely defeated, but brought to ruin. The truth is, that in a free country the fate of a cause must depend for the time on its leaders; and if several of the foremost of these chance to stumble and fall disabled at nearly the same time, they leave their followers helpless. Now, the more strenuous lovers of peace had placed their trust in four men; and it might seem, at first sight, that any political cause would at least be safe from ruin when under the charge of Lord Aberdeen the Prime Minister, Mr Gladstone the Chancellor of the Exchequer, and, besides these, Mr Cobden and Mr Bright, two of the most gifted orators in the country with seats in the House of Commons.

Loving peace, with a purity of motive and a devotedness of heart which no man has ever questioned, Lord Aberdeen and Mr Gladstone had the misfortune to remain members of a Government which went out of the safe paths of peace. They went wrong; and although it is true that they went wrong at a slow rate, still they so moved for a period of eight months; and at last, to their grief and dismay, they found that they had been leading the country into a cruel war. Deceived by the crude notion that France and England, acting together, could secure peace, they did not understand that the way to maintain peace and order was to hold to the alliance of the four Powers, and to avoid impairing it by a separate understanding with one of them. For want of this guiding principle they always failed to see the point at which they could make their stand, and they never could choose the day on which it would become them to retire from office. So they lingered on in a Cabinet which was becoming more and more warlike, and their presence there was in two ways hurtful to the cause of peace — for even the more earnest friends of peace were quieted by seeing that the trusted champions of the cause were still members of the Government; and at last, when they could no longer help seeing that this same Government was going to a rupture with the Czar, the more rational of them thought that there must really be some great State necessity for a war in which Lord Aberdeen and Mr Gladstone were reluctantly engaging their country. Moreover, there was a great and good portion of the community who, retaining their theoretic disapproval of a needless war, were nevertheless fired with a secret longing for the clash of arms; and these men were relieved from the pain of a conflict beween duty and inclination by finding that for the righteousness of the impending war Lord Aberdeen and Mr Gladstone were their sponsors.

It has been seen also that, by their continuance in office, these two statesmen kept alive in the mind of the Emperor Nicholas that dangerous belief which has often been a source of European troubles — the belief that England would not go to war. The Czar's belief on this subject was so sweet to him, that perhaps nothing short of the resignation of the Prime Minister could have undeceived him. Still, to a common observer, it would seem that some effort might have been made to disperse the error which Lord Aberdeen and Mr Gladstone had graven into the mind of the Czar by consenting to remain in office; and that, as the danger was caused in great measure by the continuance of old impressions upon the mind of the Emperor Nicholas, a special mission to St Petersburg might have been usefully resorted to as a means of rousing the Czar to a sense of the danger which was threatening his relations with England. Nothing of this kind was done; nothing was done to break the fatal smoothness of the incline.

But if the cause of peace was paralysed by the friends whom it had in the Cabinet, it was brought to mere extinction by the disqualification inflicted upon its popular leaders as the result of their former excesses.

Mr Cobden and Mr Bright, as we have seen, had shut themselves out from the counsels of the nation. They were powerless. By their indiscriminate denunciations of war in general, they had destroyed the worth of any criticism which they might be able to bring to bear upon the pending dispute. Their arguments, however well pruned and shaped out to suit the occasion, were sure of being treated by an English audience as the offspring of their doctrines; and their doctrines being repudiated, they could make no good use of their privilege of speech. It was impossible to consult with them upon the question whether the country was bound in honour to take up arms for the Sultan, because they had spent their lives in teaching that the country could never be bound in honour to take up arms for anybody. If they had not thus disqualified themselves for useful argument, they would surely have been able to make a becoming stand against what Count Nesselrode called "the most unintelligible war" ever known. But because they had been extravagant before, therefore now they were null; and because they were null, the cause intrusted to their hands was brought to destruction.

The whole Cabinet of Lord Aberdeen must share the responsibility of that ill-fated policy which brought England to cast aside the blessings insured by the unanimity of the four Powers, and to enter into a separate understanding with France. It is true that, because this policy was novel and adventurous, it was highly approved by a people glowing with warlike ardour, and seeking for fields of enterprise; but although for the time an Administration may be thus borne harmless, it would be wrong to allow that in questions of high policy the complicity of the public has power to absolve. A Minister who has fashioned out a new policy leading his country into a war ought to be able to show — not necessarily that the policy was a wise one (for man is of an erring nature), but — that at the time of its adoption there were better grounds than its mere popularity for believing it to be right. That some such grounds exist may be fairly imagined by those who have heard of the ability and the varied experience of the members of Lord Aberdeen's Cabinet; but hitherto, so far as I know, these grounds have not been disclosed.

Again, blame attaches upon Lord Aberdeen's Cabinet for yielding up its own better judgment under pressure from the French Government, and consenting to those hostile movements of the Allied fleets which baffled the patient labours of diplomacy, and twice rekindled the strife. When the warlike spirit in England had once arisen, the French Emperor knew that he could at any moment subject Lord Aberdeen's Cabinet to an access of popular disfavour by causing or allowing it to appear in England that the Government of the Queen was less eager than himself in the defence of the Sultan; and it is true, therefore, that although the hand which touched the lever was foreign, the instrument of pressure was English. It is probably true, also, that the pressure was never inflicted without the consent of at least one great English Statesman. Still, because this facile yielding to the French Emperor in the use of naval forces was popular, or rather was a means of avoiding unpopularity, the propriety of it is not the less in question. It is possible, however, that the hitherto unknown grounds on which the separate understanding with France may come to be defended will extend to justify the plan of deferring in naval transactions to the Emperor of the French, and consenting at his instance to make our fleet an instrument for the disturbance of the pending negotiations.

In so far as concerns the general policy of the Government in these transactions, the merits of Lord Clarendon must be tried, of course, by the tests applicable to the whole body of the Cabinet; but it has been seen that, personally, he was not blind to the danger of allowing the Czar to continue in his belief of England's insuperable peacefulness; and that his firm, wholesome words were flying, as they say, to St Petersburg* when unhappily they were revoked at the instance of Lord Aberdeen. Lord Clarendon's despatches were written with so much of grace and vigour, and in a tone so fair and manly, that any one who is familiar with them will understand something of the process by which Lord Aberdeen was from time to time forced into an approval of these able writings, and in that way hindered from finding the happy moment in which he could establish his divergence from the governing member of the Cabinet and effect his retreat from office.

---

* I have avoided the obvious step by which this statement might be verified or disproved, because it seemed to me that a question upon the subject would be hardly fair; and I have preferred, therefore, to give it under cover of the ὡς φασιν. I do not, however, doubt that it is true.

Looking back upon the troubles which ended in the outbreak of war, one sees the nations at first swaying backward and forward like a throng so vast as to be helpless, but afterwards falling slowly into warlike array. And when one begins to search for the man or the men whose volition was governing the crowd, the eye falls upon the towering form of the Emperor Nicholas. He was not single-minded, and therefore his will was unstable, but it had a huge force; and since he was armed with the whole authority of his Empire, it seemed plain that it was this man, and only he, who was bringing danger from the North. And at first, too, it seemed that within his range of action there was none who could be his equal; but in a little while the looks of men were turned to the Bosphorus, for thither his ancient adversary was slowly bending his way. To fit him for the encounter, the Englishman was clothed with little authority except what he could draw from the resources of his own mind and from the strength of his own wilful nature. Yet it was presently seen that those who were near him fell under his dominion, and did as he bid them, and that the circle of deference to his will was always increasing around him; and soon it appeared that, though he moved gently, he began to have mastery over a foe who was consuming his strength in mere anger. When he had conquered, he stood, as it were, with folded arms, and seemed willing to desist from strife. But

CHAP. XXVIII.
The volitions which governed events.

CHAP.
XXVIII.

also in the West there had been seen a knot of men possessed, for the time, of the mighty engine of the French State, and striving so to use it as to be able to keep their hold, and to shelter themselves from a cruel fate. The volitions of these men were active enough, because they were toiling for their lives. Their efforts seemed to interest and to please the lustiest man of those days, for he watched them from over the Channel with approving smile, and began to declare, in his good-humoured, boisterous way, that so long as they should be suffered to have the handling of France, so long as they would execute for him his policy, so long as they would take care not to deceive him, they ought to be encouraged, they ought to be made use of, they ought to have the shelter they wanted; and, the Frenchmen agreeing to his conditions, he was willing to level the barrier — he called it, perhaps, false pride — which divided the Government of the Queen from the venturers of the 2d of December. In this thought, at the moment, he stood almost alone; but he abided his time. At length he saw the spring of 1853, bringing with it grave peril to the Ottoman State. Then, throwing aside with a laugh some papers which belonged to the Home Office, he gave his strong shoulder to the levelling work. Under the weight of his touch the barrier fell. Thenceforth the hindrances that met him were but slight. As he from the first had willed it, so moved the two great nations of the West.

APPENDIX.

PART I.

PAPERS SHOWING THE DIFFERENCE WHICH LED TO THE RUPTURE OF PRINCE MENTSCHIKOFF'S NEGOTIATION.

Draft of Note proposed by Prince Mentschikoff to be addressed to him by the Porte.*

La Sublime Porte, après l'examen le plus attentif et le plus sérieux des demandes qui forment l'objet de la mission extraordinaire confiée à l'Ambassadeur de Russie, Prince Mentschikoff, et après avoir soumis le résultat de cet examen à Sa Majesté le Sultan, se fait un devoir empressé de notifier par la présente à son Altesse l'Ambassadeur la décision Impériale émanée à ce sujet par un Iradé suprême en date du   (date Musulmane et Chrétienne).

Sa Majesté voulant donner à son auguste allié et ami l'Empereur de Russie un nouveau témoignage de son amitié la plus sincère, et de son désir intime de consolider les anciennes relations de bon voisinage et de parfaite entente qui existent entre les deux Etats, plaçant en même temps une entière confiance dans les intentions constam-

---

* This was the last demand made by the Prince.

ment bienveillantes de Sa Majesté Impériale pour le maintien de l'intégrité et de l'indépendance de l'Empire Ottoman, a daigné apprécier et prendre en sérieuse considération les représentations franches et cordiales dont l'Ambassadeur de Russie s'est rendu l'organe en faveur du culte orthodoxe Gréco-Russe professé par son auguste allié ainsi que par la majorité de leurs sujets respectifs.

Le Soussigné a reçu en conséquence l'ordre de donner par la présente note, l'assurance la plus solennelle au Gouvernement de Russie, que représente auprès de Sa Majesté le Sultan, son Altesse le Prince Mentschikoff, sur la sollicitude invariable et les sentiments généreux et tolérans qui animent Sa Majesté le Sultan pour la sécurité et la prospérité dans ses états du clergé, des églises, et des établissements religieux du culte Chrétien d'Orient.

Afin de rendre ces assurances plus explicites, préciser d'une manière formelle les objets principaux de cette haute sollicitude, corroborer par des éclaircissements supplémentaires que nécessite la marche du temps, le sens des Articles qui dans les Traités antérieurs conclus entre les deux Puissances ont trait aux questions religieuses, et prévenir enfin à jamais toute nuance de malentendu et de désaccord à ce sujet entre les deux Gouvernements, le Soussigné est autorisé par Sa Majesté le Sultan à faire les déclarations suivantes:

1. Le culte orthodoxe d'Orient, son clergé, ses églises, et ses possessions, ainsi que ses établissements religieux, jouiront dans l'avenir sans aucune atteinte, sous l'égide de Sa Majesté le Sultan, des privilèges et immunités qui leur sont assurés *ab antiquo*, ou qui leur ont été accordés à différentes reprises par la faveur Impérial, et dans un principe de haute équité participeront aux avantages accordés aux autres rites Chrétiens, ainsi qu'aux Légations Etrangères

accréditées près la Sublime Porte par Convention ou disposition particulière.

2. Sa Majesté le Sultan ayant jugé nécessaire et équitable de corroborer et d'expliquer son firman souverain revêtu du hattihoumayoum le 15 de la lune de Rebiul-Akhir 1268 (10 Février, 1852), par son firman souverain du   et d'ordonner en sus par un autre firman en date du   la réparation de la coupole du Temple du Saint Sépulcre, ces deux firmans seront textuellement exécutés et fidèlement observés, pour maintenir à jamais le *status quo* actuel des sanctuaires possédés par les Grecs exclusivement ou en commun avec d'autres cultes.

Il est entendu que cette promesse s'étend également au maintien de tous les droits et immunités dont jouissent *ab antiquo* l'église orthodoxe et son clergé tant dans la ville de Jérusalem qu'au-déhors, sans aucun préjudice pour les autres communautés Chrétiennes.

3. Pour le cas où la Cour Impériale de Russie en ferait la demande, il sera assigné une localité convenable dans la ville de Jérusalem ou dans les environs pour la construction d'une église consacrée à la célébration du service divin par les ecclésiastiques Russes, et d'un hospice pour les pèlerins indigents ou malades, lesquelles fondations seront sous la surveillance spéciale du Consulat-Général de Russie en Syrie et en Palestine.

4. On donnera les firmans et les ordres nécessaires à qui de droit et aux Patriarches Grecs pour l'exécution de ces décisions souveraines, et on s'entendra ultérieurement sur la régularisation des points de détail qui n'auront pas trouvé place tant dans les firmans concernant les lieux saints de Jérusalem que dans la présente notification.

Le Soussigné, &c.

Reshid Pasha to Prince Mentschikoff.*

(Translation.)

The statement made by Prince Mentschikoff, in his written and verbal communications, concerning the doubts and want of confidence entertained by the Porte with regard to His Majesty the Emperor's good intentions, has been seen with great regret. His Majesty the Sultan has perfect faith and confidence in His Majesty the Emperor, and highly appreciates the great qualities and spirit of justice which animate his august ally and neighbour, and it is a great honour for me to proclaim that it has always been His Majesty the Sultan's desire to consolidate and strengthen the friendly relations happily subsisting between the two countries.

With reference to the religious privileges of the Greek churches and clergy, the honour of the Porte requires that the exclusively spiritual privileges granted under the Sultan's predecessors, and confirmed by His Majesty, should be now and henceforward preserved unimpaired and in force; and the equitable system pursued by the Porte towards its subjects demands that any spiritual privilege whatever granted henceforward to one class of Christian subjects should not be refused to the Greek clergy. It would be a cause of much regret that the fixed intentions of His Majesty the Sultan in this respect should be called into question.

Nevertheless, the imperial firman now granted to the Greek Patriarchate, confirming the religious privileges, is considered to afford a new proof of His Imperial Majesty's

---

* This was the last offer made by the Porte to Prince Mentschikoff.

benevolent sentiments in this respect, and the general promulgation thereof must afford every security, and remove for ever from His Imperial Majesty's mind all doubts for the future respecting the religion which he professes, and it is with pleasure that I perform the duty of making this declaration.

In order that there should be no alteration respecting the Shrine at Jerusalem, it is formally promised that for security in the future thereon the Sublime Porte will take no step concerning them without the knowledge of the French and Russian Governments. An official note has been addressed to the French Embassy also to this purpose.

The Sultan consents that a church and hospital should be built at Jerusalem (for the Russians); and the Porte is ready and disposed to conclude a Sened, both on this subject and concerning the special privileges of the Russian monks at that place.

PART II.

THE "VIENNA NOTE," WITH THE PROPOSED TURKISH MODIFICATIONS, SHOWING THE POINTS OF THE DIFFERENCE, WHICH WAS FOLLOWED BY WAR BETWEEN RUSSIA AND TURKEY.

Copy of the Vienna Projet de Note, as modified by the Sublime Porte.

[The Turkish modifications are shown by printing in Italics the words which the Porte rejected, and placing the words which it proposed to substitute in the foot-note.]

Sa Majesté le Sultan n'ayant rien de plus à cœur que de rétablir entre elle et Sa Majesté l'Empereur de Russie les relations de bon voisinage et de parfaite entente qui ont été malheureusement altérées par de récentes et pénibles complications, a pris soigneusement à tâcher de rechercher les moyens d'effacer les traces de ce différend.

Un irade suprême en date du   lui ayant fait connaître la décision Impériale, la Sublime Porte se félicite de pouvoir la communiquer à son Excellence M. le Comte de Nesselrode.

Si à toute époque les Empereurs de Russie ont témoigné leur active sollicitude pour *le maintien des immunités et privilèges de l'Eglise Orthodoxe Grecque dans l'Empire Ottoman,* les Sultans ne se sont jamais refusés à les consacrer* de nouveau par des actes solennels qui attestaient de leur ancienne et constante bienveillance à l'égard de leurs sujets Chrétiens.

Sa Majesté le Sultan Abdul-Medjid, aujourd'hui régnant, animé des mêmes dispositions et voulant donner à Sa Majesté l'Empereur de Russie un témoignage personnel de son amitié la plus sincère, n'a écouté que sa confiance infinie dans les qualités éminentes de son auguste ami et allié, et a daigné prendre en sérieuse considération les représentations dont son Altesse le Prince de Mentschikoff s'est rendu l'organe auprès de la Sublime Porte.

Le Soussigné a reçu en conséquence l'ordre de déclarer par la présente que le Gouvernement de Sa Majesté le Sultan restera fidèle *à la lettre et à l'esprit des stipulations des Traités de Kainardji et d'Andrinople, relatives à la protection du culte Chrétien*,** et que Sa Majesté regarde comme étant de son honneur de faire observer à tout jamais, et de préserver de toute atteinte, soit présentement, soit dans l'avenir, la jouissance des privilèges spirituels qui ont été accordés par les augustes aïeux de Sa Majesté à l'Eglise Orthodoxe de l'Orient, qui sont maintenus et confirmés par elle; et, en outre, à faire participer dans un esprit de haute équité le rit Grec aux avantages *concédés aux autres rits Chrétiens par Convention ou disposition particulière*.***

---

* Le culte et l'Eglise Orthodoxe Grecque, les Sultans n'ont jamais cessé de veiller au maintien des immunités et privilèges qu'ils ont spontanément accordés à diverses reprises à ce culte et à cette Eglise dans l'Empire Ottoman, et de les consacrer.

** Aux stipulations du Traité de Kainardji confirmé par celui d'Andrinople, relatives à la protection par la Sublime Porte de la religion Chrétienne, et il est en outre chargé de faire connaître.

*** Octroyés, ou qui seraient octroyés, aux autres communautés Chrétiennes, sujettes Ottomanes.

Au reste, comme le firman Impérial qui vient d'être donné au patriarcat et au clergé Grec, et qui contient les confirmations de leurs privilèges spirituels, devra être regardé comme une nouvelle preuve de ses nobles sentiments, et comme, en outre, la proclamation de ce firman, qui donne toute sécurité, devra faire disparaître toute crainte à l'égard du rit qui est la religion de Sa Majesté l'Empereur de Russie; je suis heureux d'être chargé du devoir de faire la présente notification.

PART III.

PAPERS SHOWING THE CONCORD EXISTING BETWEEN THE FOUR POWERS AT THE TIME WHEN FRANCE AND ENGLAND WERE ENGAGING IN A SEPARATE COURSE OF ACTION.

Protocol of a Conference held at Vienna, February 2, 1854.

(Translation.)

Present: The Representatives of Austria, France, Great Britain, and Prussia.

The Representatives of Austria, France, Great Britain, and Prussia, have met together in conference to hear the communication which the Austrian Plenipotentiary has been good enough to make to them of the propositions submitted by the Cabinet of St Petersburg in reply to those which he had undertaken, on the 13th of January, to forward to the Imperial Government, and which were sanctioned by the approval of the Powers represented in the Conference of Vienna. The document which contains them is annexed to the present Protocol.

The Undersigned, after having submitted the above-mentioned propositions to the most careful examination, have ascertained that, in their general character and in their details, they so essentially differ from the basis of negotiation agreed upon on the 31st of December at Constantinople, and approved on the 13th January at Vienna, that they have not considered them to be such as should be forwarded to the Government of His Imperial Majesty the Sultan.

It consequently only remains for the Undersigned to transmit the annexed document to their respective Courts, and to wait till they shall have taken their final resolutions.

    (Signed) BUOL-SCHAUENSTEIN
           BOURQUENEY.
           WESTMORLAND.
           ARNIM.

The Earl of Westmorland to the Earl of Clarendon. — (Received February 13.)*

Vienna, February 5, 1853.

MY LORD,

I HAVE just left the Conference to which Count Buol had this morning invited me, in conjunction with my colleagues. Upon our assembling, he stated that he had no proposal to make to us; but, in consideration of the perfect union existing amongst us upon the Eastern Question, he thought he was forwarding our common objects by communicating the despatches he had addressed to Count Esterhazy, for the purpose of being submitted to Count Nesselrode.

Count Buol then read to us these despatches. The first gave an account of the proposal brought forward by Count

---

* *i. e.*, just one fortnight before England despatched the hostile summons which brought her into a state of war.

Orloff, that the Emperor of Austria should, in conjunction with Prussia, take an engagement with the Emperor of Russia for the maintenance of a strict neutrality in the war now existing with the Porte, and in which the Maritime Powers seemed likely to take part. Count Buol, in his despatch, developes in the clearest and most distinct language the impossibility of the adoption by the Emperor of any such engagement. He states, with all courtesy to the Emperor Nicholas, the obligations by which the Austrian Government is bound to watch over the strict maintenance of the principle of the independence and integrity of Turkey—a principle proclaimed by the Emperor Nicholas himself, but which the passage of the Danube by his troops might, by the encouragement of insurrections in the Turkish Provinces, endanger. Count Buol, therefore, states that he cannot take the engagement proposed to him. The second despatch to Count Esterhazy relates to the answer which has been returned to the proposals for negotiations transmitted by Count Buol with the sanction of the Conference on the 13th ultimo.

In this despatch, Count Buol states with considerable force the disappointment felt by the Emperor at the want of success which had attended his recommendation in favour of the Turkish propositions. He enters very fully into the subject, and renews the expression of the Emperor's most anxious desire that the Emperor Nicholas may still adopt the proposals which had been submitted to him.

The last despatch is one in which Count Buol replies to the reproach which was addressed to the Imperial Government, that by its present conduct it was abandoning the principles upon which the three governments of Russia, Austria, and Prussia, had hitherto acted for the maintenance of the established interests and independence of the different States of Europe, and that, by so doing, it was endangering the established order of things in Europe, and the security at present existing.

The answer of Count Buol to this reproach is very firmly and clearly stated.

It is impossible for me to give your Lordship a more detailed account, before the departure of the messenger, of these despatches; but I must add, that they met with the entire approbation of the members of the Conference, that they were looked upon as most ably drawn up, and that while using every courteous and friendly expression towards the Emperor Nicholas, they most clearly pointed out the present position which the Austrian Government would maintain with the view of upholding the principles they had proclaimed, and the engagements which they had taken for their support.*

Protocol of a Conference held at Vienna, March 5, 1854.**

(Translation.)

Present: the Representatives of Austria, France, Great Britain, and Prussia.

THE undersigned, Representatives of Austria, France, Great Britain, and Prussia, having again met in Conference on the summons of the Austrian Plenipotentiary, the

---

* The rest of the despatch relates only to a suggestion for an arrangement which came to nothing, and is therefore omitted.

** *i. e.*, whilst messengers were carrying the hostile summons from Paris and London to St Petersburg.

annexed document which had been communicated to the Cabinet of Vienna by the Envoy of Russia, and which contains the preliminaries of the Treaty to be concluded between Russia and the Porte, was read to them, the Court of Austria being requested by the Cabinet of St Petersburg to apply for the support of the two Maritime Powers, in order to obtain the acceptance of these preliminaries by the Sublime Porte.

After mature deliberation, the Plenipotentiaries of France and Great Britain, taking as the basis of their examination the previous documents which had received the sanction of the four Powers, established the existence of radical differences between those documents and the proposed preliminaries.

1. Inasmuch as the evacuation of the Danubian Principalities, which is fixed to take place after the signature of the preliminaries, is made to depend on the departure of the combined fleets, not only from the Black Sea but from the Straits of the Bosphorus and of the Dardanelles, a condition which could only be admitted by the Maritime Powers after the conclusion of the definitive Treaty.

2. Inasmuch as the document now under consideration tends to invest with a form strictly conventional, bilateral, and exclusively applicable to the relations of the Porte with Russia, the assurances relative to the religious privileges of the Greeks — assurances which the Porte has only offered to give to the five Powers at the same time and in the form of a simple identic declaration. The assurances, in fact, once inserted in the preliminary Treaty, must then needs be reproduced in the definitive Treaty, and would be accompanied, moreover, by an official note confirmatory of the said privileges exclusively addressed to the Court of Russia, a note which, in its turn, would be considered as

annexed to the Treaties; that is to say, as having the same force and the same effect.

3. Inasmuch as the preliminaries communicated to Vienna are, by implication, withheld from any discussion in Conference upon the modifications considered necessary to make them correspond with the original text of the Acts which had received its assent, and inasmuch as the conclusion of the definitive Treaty contains no greater reservation for its inspection and interference.

4. Inasmuch as, whilst the propositions of the Porte expressly require the revision of the Treaty of 1841, so as to make Turkey participate in the guarantees of the public law of Europe, this condition is passed over in silence.

The Plenipotentiaries of Austria and Prussia, appreciating the force of the observations offered by the Plenipotentiaries of France and of Great Britain, recognised in like manner on their part the remarkable differences pointed out between the Russian draft of preliminaries and the Protocols of the 13th of January and 2d of February.

In consequence, the Conference unanimously agreed that it was impossible to proceed with those propositions.

    (Signed) BUOL-SCHAUENSTEIN.
           BOURQUENEY.
           WESTMORLAND.
           ARNIM.

APPENDIX. 265

Protocol of a Conference held at Vienna, April 9, 1854.*

(Translation.)

Present: The Representatives of Austria, France, Great Britain, and Prussia.

At the request of the Plenipotentiaries of France and of Great Britain, the Conference met to hear the documents read which establish that the invitation addressed to the Cabinet of St Petersburg to evacuate the Moldo-Wallachian provinces within a fixed time having remained unanswered, the state of war already declared between Russia and the Sublime Porte is in actual existence equally between Russia on the one side, and France and Great Britain on the other.

This change which has taken place in the attitude of two of the Powers represented at the Conference of Vienna, in consequence of a step taken directly by France and England, supported by Austria and Prussia as being founded in right, has been considered by the Representatives of Austria and Prussia as involving the necessity of a fresh declaration of the union of the four Powers upon the ground of the principles laid down in the Protocols of December 5, 1853, and January 13, 1854.

In consequence, the Undersigned have at this solemn moment declared that their Governments remain united in the double object of maintaining the territorial integrity of the Ottoman Empire, of which the fact of the evacuation of the Danubian Principalities is and will remain one of the essential conditions; and of consolidating in an interest so

* i. e., the very day before the Treaty of Alliance between England and France.

much in conformity with the sentiments of the Sultan, and by every means compatible with his independence and sovereignty, the civil and religious rights of the Christian subjects of the Porte.

The territorial integrity of the Ottoman Empire is and remains the *sine quâ non* condition of every transaction having for its object the re-establishment of peace between the belligerent Powers; and the governments represented by the Undersigned engage to endeavour in common to discover the guarantees most likely to attach the existence of that Empire to the general equilibrium of Europe; as they also declare themselves ready to deliberate and to come to an understanding as to the employment of the means calculated to accomplish the object of their agreement.

Whatever event may arise in consequence of this agreement, founded solely upon the general interests of Europe, and of which the object can only be attained by the return of a firm and lasting peace, the Governments represented by the Undersigned reciprocally engage not to enter into any definitive arrangements with the Imperial Court of Russia, or with any other Power, which would be at variance with the principles above enunciated, without previously deliberating thereon in common.

(Signed)   BUOL-SCHAUENSTEIN.
BOURQUENEY.
WESTMORLAND.
ARNIM.

Treaty of Alliance, Offensive and Defensive, between Austria and Prussia.

(Translation.)

His Majesty the Emperor of Austria, and His Majesty the King of Prussia, penetrated with deep regret at the fruitlessness of their attempts hitherto to prevent the breaking out of war between Russia, on the one hand, and Turkey, France, and England, on the other;

Mindful of the moral obligations entered into by them by the signing of the last Vienna Protocol;

In the face of the military measures ever gathering on both sides around them, and of the dangers resulting therefrom for the general peace of Europe;

Convinced of the high duty which on the threshold of a future pregnant with evil, is imposed, in the interest of the European welfare, on Germany, so intimately united with the States of the two High Parties;

Have determined to ally themselves in an offensive and defensive alliance for the duration of the war which has broken out between Russia, on the one hand, and Turkey, France, and England, on the other, and have appointed for the conclusion of it the following Plenipotentiaries:

His Majesty the Emperor of Austria, the Baron Henry de Hess, his actual Privy Councillor, &c. &c.; and the Count de Frederick de Thun-Hohenstein, his Chamberlain, actual Privy Councillor, &c. &c.;

And His Majesty the King of Prussia, the Baron Otho Theodore de Manteuffel, his President of the Council of Ministers, and Minister for Foreign Affairs, &c. &c.

The same having exchanged their full powers found to be in good order, have agreed upon the following points:

Article I.

His Imperial Apostolic Majesty and His Majesty the King of Prussia guarantee to each other reciprocally the possession of their German and non-German possessions, so that an attack made on the territory of the one, from whatever quarter, will be regarded by the other as an act of hostility against his own territory.

Article II.

In the same manner, the High Contracting Parties hold themselves engaged to defend the rights and interests of Germany against all and every injury, and consider themselves bound accordingly for the mutual repulse of every attack on any part whatsoever of their territories; likewise also in the case where one of the two may find himself, in understanding with the other, obliged to advance actively for the defence of German interests. The agreement relating to the latter-named eventuality, as likewise the extent of the assistances then to be given, will form a special, as also integral, part of the present Convention.

Article III.

In order also to give due security and force to the conditions of the offensive and defensive alliance now concluded, the two Great German Powers bind themselves, in case of need, to hold in perfect readiness for war a part of their forces, at periods to be determined between them and in positions to be fixed. With respect to the time, the extent, and the nature of the placing of those troops, a special stipulation will likewise be determined.

Article IV.

The High Contracting Parties will invite all the German Governments of the Confederation to accede to this alliance, with the understanding that the federal obligations existing in virtue of Article 47 of the final Act of Vienna will receive the same extension for the States who accede as the present Treaty stipulates.

Article V.

Neither of the two High Contracting Parties will, during the duration of this alliance, enter into any separate alliance with other Powers which shall not be in entire harmony with the basis of the present treaty.

Article VI.

The present Convention shall be ratified as soon as possible by the High Contracting Sovereigns.

Done at Berlin, April 20, 1854.*

    (L.S.)   Henry Bon. de Hess.
    (L.S.)   F. Thun.
    (L.S.)   Bon. Oth. Theod. Manteuffel.

* i. e., ten days after the date of the Anglo-French alliance.

(Translation.)

Additional Article to the Offensive and Defensive Alliance between Austria and Prussia of April 20, 1854.

According to the conditions of Article II. of the Treaty concluded this day between His Imperial Majesty the Emperor of Austria, and His Majesty the King of Prussia, for the establishment of an offensive and defensive alliance, a more intimate understanding with respect to the eventuality when an active advance of one of the High Contracting Parties may impose on the other the obligation of a mutual protection of the territory of both, was to form the subject of a special agreement to be considered as an integral part of the Treaty.

Their Majesties have not been able to divest themselves of the consideration, that the indefinite continuance of the occupation of the territories on the Lower Danube, under the sovereignty of the Ottoman Porte, by Imperial Russian troops, would endanger the political, moral, and material interests of the whole German Confederation, as also of their own States, and the more so in proportion as Russia extends her warlike operations on Turkish territory.

The Courts of Austria and Prussia are united in the desire to avoid every participation in the war which has broken out between Russia, on the one hand, and Turkey, France, and Great Britain, on the other, and at the same time to contribute to the restoration of general peace. They more especially consider the declarations lately made at Berlin by the Court of St Petersburg, to be an important element of pacification, the failure of the practical influence of which they would view with regret.

According to these declarations, Russia appears to regard the original motive for the occupation of the Principalities as removed by the concessions now granted to the Christian subjects of the Porte, which offer the prospect of realisation. They, therefore, hope that the replies awaited from the Cabinet of Russia to the Prussian propositions, transmitted on the 8th, will offer to them the necessary guarantee for an early withdrawal of the Russian troops. In the event that this hope should be illusory, the Plenipotentiaries named on the part of His Majesty the Emperor of Austria, Freiherr Baron von Hess and Count Thun, and on the part of His Majesty the King of Prussia, Baron Manteuffel, have drawn up the following more detailed agreement with respect to the eventuality alluded to in the above-mentioned Article II. of the Treaty of Alliance of this day:

Single Article.

The Imperial Austrian Government will also on their side address a communication to the Imperial Russian Court with the object of obtaining from the Emperor of Russia the necessary orders, that an immediate stop should be put to the further advance of his armies upon the Turkish territory, as also to request of His Imperial Majesty sufficient guarantees for the prompt evacuation of the Danubian Principalities; and the Prussian Government will again, in the most emphatic manner, support these communications with reference to their proposals already sent to St Petersburg. Should the answer of the Russian Court to these steps of the Cabinets of Vienna and Berlin — contrary to expectation — not be of a nature to give them entire satisfaction upon the two points aforementioned, the measures to be taken by one of the Contracting Parties for their attainment, according to the terms of Article II. of the Offensive and Defensive Alliance signed on this day, will be on the understanding, that every hostile attack on the territory of one of the Contracting Parties is to be repelled with all the military forces at the disposal of the other.

But a mutual offensive advance is stipulated for only in the event of the incorporation of the Principalities, or in the event of an attack on, or passage of, the Balkan by Russia.*

The present Convention shall be submitted for the ratification of the High Sovereigns simultaneously with the above-mentioned Treaty.

Done at Berlin the 28th of April 1854.

(Signed) Hess.   (Signed) Manteuffel.
          Tron.

---

* Of course the contemplated march of Austrian troops into the Principalities (though undertaken with a view to expel the Russian forces) could not be "a mutual offensive advance." The clause defines the circumstances in which the two great German sovereigns should be bound to attack Russia, and does not cast any obscurity upon that part of the treaty which provided for the event in which "one of the two may find himself in understanding with the others obliged to advance actively for the defence of German interests."

APPENDIX.

Protocol signed at Vienna on the 23d of May 1854 by the Representatives of Austria, France, Great Britain, and Prussia.

(Translation.)

Present: The Representatives of Austria, France, Great Britain, and Prussia.

The Undersigned Plenipotentiaries have deemed it conformable to the arrangements contained in the Protocol of the 9th of April, to meet in conference in order to communicate reciprocally, and record in one common Act, the Conventions concluded between France and England on the one hand, and between Austria and Prussia on the other, upon the 10th and 20th of April of the present year.

After a careful examination of the aforesaid Conventions, the Undersigned have unanimously agreed:

1. That the Convention concluded between France and England, as well as that signed on the 20th of April between Austria and Prussia, bind both of them, in the relative situations to which they apply, to secure the maintenance of the principle established by the series of Protocols of the Conference of Vienna.

2. That the integrity of the Ottoman Empire, and the evacuation of that portion of its territory which is occupied by the Russian army, are, and will continue to be, the constant and invariable object of the union of the four Powers.

3. That, consequently, the Acts communicated and annexed to the present Protocol correspond to the engage-

ment which the Plenipotentiaries had mutually contracted on the 9th of April, to deliberate and agree upon the means most fit to accomplish the object of their union, and thus give a fresh sanction to the firm intention of the four Powers represented at the Conference of Vienna, to combine all their efforts and resolutions to realise the object which forms the basis of their union.

(Signed)   BUOL-SCHAUENSTEIN.
                        BOURQUENEY.
                        WESTMORLAND.
                        ARNIM.

Convention between His Imperial Majesty the Emperor of Austria and the Ottoman Porte. Signed at Boyadji-Keuy, June 14, 1854.

(Translation.)

HIS Majesty the Emperor of Austria, fully recognising that the existence of the Ottoman Empire within its present limits is necessary for the maintenance of the balance of power between the States of Europe, and that, specifically, the evacuation of the Danubian Principalities is one of the essential conditions of the integrity of that Empire; being, moreover, ready to join, with the means at his disposal, in the measures proper to insure the object of the agreement established between his Cabinet and the High Courts represented at the Conference of Vienna:

His Imperial Majesty the Sultan having, on his side, accepted this offer of concert, made in a friendly manner by His Majesty the Emperor of Austria;

It has seemed proper to conclude a Convention, in order to regulate the manner in which the concert in question shall be carried into effect.

With this object, His Imperial Majesty the Emperor of Austria, and His Imperial Majesty the Sultan, have named as their Plenipotentiaries, that is to say:

His Majesty the Emperor of Austria, M. le Baron Charles de Bruck, Privy Councillor of His Imperial and Royal Apostolic Majesty, his Internuncio and Minister Plenipotentiary at the Sublime Ottoman Porte, Grand Cross of the Imperial Order of Leopold, Knight of the Imperial Order of the Iron Crown of the first class, &c.;

And His Imperial Majesty the Sultan, Mustapha Reshid Pasha, late Grand Vizier, and at present his Minister for Foreign Affairs, decorated with the Imperial Order of Medjidié of the first class, &c.;

Who, after having exchanged their full powers, found to be in good and due form, have agreed upon the following Articles:

Article I.

His Majesty the Emperor of Austria engages to exhaust all the means of negotiation, and all other means, to obtain the evacuation of the Danubian Principalities by the foreign army which occupies them, and even to employ, in case they are required, the number of troops necessary to attain this end.

Article II.

It will appertain in this case exclusively to the Imperial Commander-in-chief to direct the operations of his army. He will, however, always take care to inform the Commander-in-chief of the Ottoman army of his operations in proper time.

Article III.

His Majesty the Emperor of Austria undertakes, by common agreement with the Ottoman Government, to reestablish in the Principalities, as far as possible, the legal state of things such as it results from the privileges secured by the Sublime Porte in regard to the administration of those countries. The local authorities thus reconstituted shall not, however, extend their action so far as to attempt to exercise control over the Imperial army.

Article IV.

The Imperial Court of Austria further engages not to enter into any plan of accommodation with the Imperial Court of Russia which has not for its basis the sovereign rights of His Imperial Majesty the Sultan, as well as the integrity of his Empire.

Article V.

As soon as the object of the present Convention shall have been obtained by the conclusion of a Treaty of Peace between the Sublime Porte and the Court of Russia, His

Majesty the Emperor of Austria will immediately make arrangements for withdrawing his forces with the least possible delay from the territory of the Principalities. The details respecting the retreat of the Austrian troops shall form the object of a special understanding with the Sublime Porte.

Article VI.

The Austrian Government expects that the authorities of the countries temporarily occupied by the Imperial troops will afford them every assistance and facility, as well for their march, their lodging, or encampment, as for their subsistence and that of their horses, and for their communications. The Austrian Government likewise expects that every demand relating to the requirements of the service shall be complied with, which shall be addressed by the Austrian commanders, either to the Ottoman Government, through the Imperial Internunciate at Constantinople, or directly to the local authorities, unless more weighty reasons render the execution of them impossible.

It is understood that the commanders of the Imperial army will provide for the maintenance of the strictest discipline among their troops, and will respect, and cause to be respected, the properties as well as the laws, the religion, and the customs of the country.

Article VII.

The present Convention shall be ratified, and the ratifications shall be exchanged at Vienna in the space of four weeks, or earlier if possible, dating from the day of its signature.

In faith of which the respective Plenipotentiaries have signed it and set their seals to it.

Done in duplicate, for one and the same effect, at Boyadji-Keuy, the fourteenth of June, one thousand eight hundred and fifty-four.

(L.S.)   V. Bauck.   (L.S.)   Reshid.

PART IV.

NOTE TO PAGE 43.

THE condition of the French Emperor on the day of Magenta was publicly seen; but on the day of the great battle which was soon afterwards fought on the Mincio, he avoided the criticism of multitudinous eyewitnesses, and great pains were taken to make France and Europe believe that the Emperor on the day of Solferino was, not only in a state to be able to give useful orders, but was actually present on a part of the field where there was dreadful danger. "The Emperor Napoleon," said the *Moniteur*, "was, so to speak, superior to himself: everywhere he was seen, always directing the battle; every one about him shuddered at the danger which incessantly threatened him; he alone seemed to be ignorant of it." These efforts caused people in England to believe a good deal of what was represented to them; but in France their success was hindered by a practical difficulty which the French Emperor had brought upon himself by his odd love of dresses and imitative display. In the ride he took on the day of Solferino, he had chosen to be followed, not only, as might have been expected, by a numerous staff, but also by a cavalry escort, with beautiful new dresses and decorations, which went by the name of the "Cent Gardes" — "The Hundred Guards." All these horsemen — the whole Imperial staff and the cavalry escort — covered altogether a good deal of ground — ground as broad and as long as many a whole street; and if they had really intruded themselves into any part of the field where there was what may be called "fighting," then, humanly speaking, they must have undergone dreadful carnage. It so happened, however, that of all this acreage of horsemen not one was killed, and only one of the "Cent Gardes" was even touched — said by some to have been struck in a part of his dress, and warranted by the *Moniteur* to have been hit in the actual body — *Moniteur*, 29th June 1859. Here then was the practical difficulty. It had to be represented that a large mass of horsemen had been moving about all day in the thick of a most bloody battle, and yet had remained unscathed. In this stress the *Moniteur* did not hesitate. It resorted to the theory of preternatural agency. It declared that the protection which the Deity threw around the Emperor *was extended to his suite*. "La protection dont Dieu l'a couvert s'est étendue à son état-major." — *Moniteur*, 29th June 1859.

Paris laughed her laugh; and thenceforth it seems to have been understood by the more prudent of the Imperialists in France that the subject of their Master's demeanour on the day of Solferino was one which they might advantageously drop.

The process of dispelling a falsehood sometimes generates a wrong notion — a notion that the exact opposite of the falsehood so dispelled is the truth. I must guard against this. The French Emperor at Solferino conducted himself in exact accordance with what I have said in the text. "He did not so give way to fear as to prove that he had less self-control in moments of danger than the common run of peaceful citizens, but he showed that, though he had chosen to set himself heroic tasks, his temperament was ill-fitted for the hour of battle, and for the crisis of an adventure."

END OF VOL. II.